Facts about Palestine

Abdul Haqq

Published by Moonstone Minarets, 2023.

Table of Contents

To the Palestinian children killed since the Belfour Declaration of
1917.

FACTS ABOUT PALESTINE

Second edition. April 6, 2024.

ISBN: 979-8223240624

Written by Abdul Haqq.

About

In October 2023, Israel launched a severe attack and siege on Gaza. This book aims to discern facts from the propaganda, fake news, and rhetoric.

Through factual information, this book highlights the oppression, marginalization, dehumanization, killing, and displacement of Palestinians. In some cases, it highlights systemic oppression through the decades of Israeli occupation.

This book is for you if you're interested in finding out facts about what's going on in Palestine and Gaza. Most facts contain direct quotes, and all stem from reputable sources, such as human rights organizations and major news outlets.

Please note that:

- I refer to Gazans, Palestinians, and Palestinian Muslims interchangeably.

- This book was published during the ongoing attacks against Palestine in 2023-2024. Any statistics are already out-of-date.

If you like this book or learned something useful from it, please consider leaving a review online for it. This will help spread the word.

What is the Nakba?

To understand the ongoing conflict in Palestine, we need to briefly divulge into some of the historical context of the region. Wikipedia states:[1]

- Palestine existed as part of the Ottoman empire, from 1516 through to the 20th century.

- The British government "issued the Balfour Declaration in 1917, favoring the establishment of a national home for the Jewish people in Palestine."[2] Shortly thereafter, they captured Palestine.

- In 1948, the UN recommended dividing Palestine into two states: one Arab (Palestinian), and one Jewish. Jews declared the independence of Israel.

- War ensued between Israel and the nearby Arab countries. "Israel not only prevailed but also conquered far more territory of the Mandate than envisioned by the Partition Plan."[3]

- 700,000, or about 80% of all Palestinians fled or were driven out of the territory that Israel conquered, and were not allowed to return, in an event that became known as the *Nakba* ("Catastrophe") to the Palestinians."[4]

- After the war, only two parts of Palestine remained in Arab control: the West Bank (and East-Jerusalem), [...] and the Gaza Strip. [Both] were conquered by Israel during the Six-Day War in 1967. Despite international objections, Israel started to establish settlements in these occupied territories.[5]

Palestinians refer to the events of 1948 as the "nakba" (disaster, catastrophe, cataclysm). Reasons may include:[6]

- Israel declared 78% of the area previously referred to as Mandatory Palestine as the state of Israel

- At least 700,000 Palestinians fled, or were expelled out of their homes by Zionist militias

- Between 400-600 Palestinian villages were destroyed

- Israelis poisoned village wells as part of a biological warfare program, resulting in a typhoid epidemic in some areas

- Israelis looted properties to prevent Palestinian refugees from returning

- Israelis renamed several sites to Hebrew names (geographical erasure)

- Denying Palestinians the Right of Return to their homes

Some historians describe the expulsion of Palestinians as ethnic cleansing.[7] As of 2023, more than 60% of the estimated 14.3 million Palestinians are displaced.[8]

Statistics on Palestinian vs. Israeli Deaths

Al-Jazeera reports[9] that, in the period between October 7, 2023, and March 14, 2024, in Gaza, Israel killed:

- 31,490 Palestinians

- 12,300 of which are children (39%)

- 8400 of which are women (27%)

In addition, Israel injured:

- 73,439 Palestinians

- 8663 of which were children

- 6327 of which were women

In contrast, Palestinians:

- Killed 1139 people

- Injured 8730 people

The ratio of killed is 28 Palestinians for 1 Israeli.

These statistics are already out of date, as the death toll continues to rise unabated.

Investigation of Highly-Circulated Claims about the Events of October 7th

———

The October 7 Fact Check website[1] investigated several prominent claims circulating in the media about the events of October 7th itself, and subsequent events around Palestine. I included a summary of their findings below, as of publication date.

Claim: Hamas decapitated 40 babies in Kfar Aza (confirmed false)[10]

- Multiple reporters failed to confirm the claims

- The Israeli government's final death count did not include any dead babies or young children in Kfar Aza

- Some reporters retracted their previous claim that this happened

- Multiple academics agree that beheadings are not a practice Hamas engages in

Claim: Hamas cooked babies in ovens (confirmed false)[11]

- Eli Beer, president of United Hatzala, widely circulated this claim in the media

- "Two [Israeli] journalists [...] contacted officials in the IDF, Shura army base, and Zaka (a volunteer organization that also deals with bodies where they are found), who said they were not familiar with the incident."

- "Eventually, Ha'aretz reported that United Hatzala, Beer's organization acknowledged the story is untrue."

- "The final death count from October 7 included one 9-month old baby (Mila Cohen) and a toddler (Omer Siman-tov 2 or 4 years old). Both were with their families when they died. Neither were found in an oven."

Claim: The IDF Killed Israeli Civilians on October 7th (confirmed true)[12]

- "There is absolutely no room for doubt that the IDF killed multiple Israeli civilians during the events of October 7th"

- "Despite initial reports implying that Hamas militants caused the vast majority of the damage in kibbutzim on October 7th, the reality is that IDF forces also caused significant structural damage and multiple civilian casualties."

- "Statements from at least two hostages that escaped captivity on October 7th confirm they were attacked by IDF forces while being kidnapped. One was explicitly fired on by an IDF helicopter. This resulted in the deaths of hostages, as both the accounts state."

- "Reporting by the Times of Israel confirms that large portions of the IDF casualties suffered in the Gaza strip since October 7th have occurred in friendly fire incidents." The articles state "20 out of 105 soldiers" and "29 of 170 soldiers" are killed by the IDF.

- "IDF ground forces in Gaza killed three hostages who were holding a white flag in a December incident." (see next claim)

Claim: Israel executed people waving white flags (confirmed true)

SEE THE SECTION "ISRAELI forces executed people waving white flags."

Claim: Hamas cut open the stomach of a pregnant woman and beheaded the baby (confirmed false)

- "An analysis of the 97-person death toll in Be'eri by the New York Times does not mention the killing of a pregnant woman, but does note that the youngest victim of the attacks was "less than a year old.""

- "The same Haaretz review reveals information contradicting the claim that the pregnant woman was found in House 426: House 426 is in the Ashelim neighborhood, which largely houses kibbutz veterans – older people. House 426 is also a two-family house where elderly families lived; Rafi Mordo was murdered and his neighbor, Simcha Shani, was wounded...Shani and her husband did not mention a pregnant woman or a family with young children who were guests in their house."

- "Fact-checking by the Anti-Defamation League, Misbar, AltNews, and FakeReporter determined that the [widely-shared] graphic video shared online was not a video of the pregnant victim and her baby. The video shows what seems to be a graphic murder by members of a Mexican cartel and was posted online in 2018 by a blog on the Mexican drug war."

Claim: Hamas kept child hostages in cages (confirmed false)

ACCORDING TO OCTOBER 7 Fact Check:[13]

• "In the days following the Oct 7 attacks, social media users widely shared a video of children in cages with captions alleging that the children were Israeli hostages held by Hamas. As of mid-October, the claim has been debunked by a range of sources including FakeReporter, France24 and Snopes.com. The video was originally posted before Oct 7 and appears to originate from a Palestinian TikTok user who has claimed that the children in the video are his relatives."

• "TikTok user @user6903068251281 posted the video before Oct 7. According to the Israeli watchdog group FakeReporter, the video was posted on Oct 4 or earlier. Palestinian news outlet Kashif identifies the TikTok user as Palestinian."

Israel is Accused of Commiting Genocide Against Palestinians

Based on rhetoric by Israeli leaders, as well as the actions of the state and army of Israel, many experts have called the actions of Israel as intentional genocide.

In October 2023, "Over 800 scholars and practitioners of international law, conflict studies and genocide studies signed a public statement warning of the possibility of genocide being perpetrated by Israeli forces against Palestinians in the Gaza Strip."[14]

The International Court of Justice ruled in January 2024 that "it is 'plausible' that Israel has committed acts that violate the Genocide Convention."[15]

Justice For All's landmark report on Palestine details the ongoing case for Palestinians being subject to genocide; you can read it here[1]. The report also begins with this statement:[16]

"What is happening in Gaza right now is a textbook case of how genocide happens. The dehumanization of Palestinians is leading to their annihilation. We ask for an immediate ceasefire, the restoration of water, food, and fuel, the end of apartheid, and freedom for the Palestinian people. We ask the USA and its European allies to commit to freedom, equal rights, and dignity for both Palestinians and Israelis.

"At the request of Justice For All the following three Nobel Peace Laureates signed the above statement:

- Mairead Maguire, Nobel Peace Prize 1976, Ireland

- Tawakkol Karman, Nobel Peace Prize 2011, Yemen

---

1. https://www.justiceforallcanada.org/pal-genocide.html

● Adolfo Pérez Esquivel, Nobel Peace Prize 1980, Argentina"

TIME writes: "Raz Segal, the program director of genocide studies at Stockton University, concretely says it is a "textbook case of genocide." Segal believes that Israeli forces are completing three genocidal acts, including, "killing, causing serious bodily harm, and measures calculated to bring about the destruction of the group." He points to the mass levels of destruction and total siege of basic necessities—like water, food, fuel, and medical supplies—as evidence."[17]

Vox writes: "On October 28, the director of the New York office of the UN High Commissioner for Human Rights stepped down because, as he wrote in his resignation letter, "we are seeing a genocide unfolding before our eyes [in Gaza] and the Organization that we serve appears powerless to stop it."[18]

AP News writes: "The Organization of Islamic Cooperation [...] said there was 'mass genocide being perpetrated by the Israeli defense forces' [...] The OIC is a block of 57 countries that include Iran, Iraq, Saudi Arabia, Qatar, and Egypt."[19]

CBC News writes: "Canadian Palestinian Muhannad Ayyash is a professor of sociology at Mount Royal University who studies violence and colonialism. He says what's happening in Gaza is "a deliberate genocidal operation" and that Canada is complicit by having not called for a ceasefire."[20]

Israeli Forces Killed Palestinian Children

According to the Internationally accepted rules of armed conflict mentioned in the Geneva Convention in 1949, which were ratified by Israel in 1951, children must be protected and treated humanely.[21]

Wikipedia states: "In the 1987-1993 Palestinian uprising against Israel, "the Israeli army killed from 1162 to 1204 (or 1,284) Palestinians, 241/332 being children."[22] That amounts to between 21-27% of all Palestinians killed.

B'Tselem statistics record 2869 Palestinian children killed from September 29, 2000 to October 6, 2023.[23] This accounts for around 21% of all deaths in that period.

Al-Jazeera reports that in the period spanning from October 7th, 2023 to March 14th, 2024, according to the UN Office for the Coordination of Humanitarian Affairs (OCHA), 12,300 children were killed (39% of the total death toll of more than 7000 and rising).[24]

Additionally, Justice for All reports[25] that over 1000 children lost one or both of their legs. With hospitals crippled, many amputations are done without anaesthetic.[26]

Israel Interrogates, Tortures, and Cages Children

Palestinian children are routinely tortured. Save the Children published an article in 2023 with harrowing statistics:[27]

- During arrest, 42% of children were injured, including gunshot wounds and broken bones

- 65% of children were arrested during the night, mostly between midnight and dawn

- Half of all arrests took place in the children's home.

- The majority of children experienced appalling levels of physical and emotional abuse, including being beaten (86%), being threatened with harm (70%), and hit with sticks or guns (60%).

- Some children reported violence and abuse of a sexual nature, including being hit or touched on the genitals and 69% reported being strip searched.

- 60% of children experienced solitary confinement with the length of time varying from one 1 day to as long as 48 days.

- 70% said they suffered from hunger

- 68% said they didn't receive any healthcare

- 58% of children were denied visits or communication with their family while detained

- The majority of children detained are boys [...] 97% of the [survey] respondents.

Children are increasingly unable to fully return to their normal life following release from detention, with the number of children having frequent nightmares rising from 39% to 53% and those suffering from insomnia or difficulty sleeping rocketing from 47% to 73%, compared to the children surveyed in 2020.[28]

A documentary by ABC Australia[29] cites the following:

- "After interrogation, children are brought here [to a military prison near Jerusalem] for trial"

- "I saw children shuffling across the courtyard, handcuffed and shackled."

- "The United Nations' childrens agency, UNICEF, [...] found that Palestinian children had been threatened with death, physical violence, solitary confinement, and sexual assault against themselves or a family member"

- The same report "found that ill-treatment was widespread, systematic, and institutionalized [...] from the moment the child was arrested, right up to the sentencing process."

- "Last month, under pressure from human rights groups, Israel stopped the long-standing practice of keeping children overnight in outdoor cages. Childrens had been kept freezing in the cages during snowstorms."

Israeli Soldiers Threw a Palestinian Boy into an Oven

According to multiple sources, including Twitter[30], Electronic Intifada[31], and Decolonize Palestine[32] Israeli soldiers threw the son of a Palestinian baker into the oven, followed by the father. All sources agree on the account. Decolonize Palestine writes:

""I saw the Zionist terrorist soldiers ordering the bakery man of the village to throw his son in the oven and burn him alive. The son is holding the clothes of his father tightly and crying from fear and pleading to his father not to do it. The father refuses and then the soldiers hit him in his gut so hard it caused him to fall on the floor. Other soldiers held his son, Abdel Rauf, and threw him in the oven and told his father to toast him well-done meat. Other soldiers took the baker himself, Hussain al-Shareef, and threw him, too, in the oven, telling him, "follow your son, he needs you there."

Israeli Forces Executed People Waving White Flags

According to October 7 Fact Check[33], the Israeli military shot and killed men, women, and children waving white flags.

"Claims that Israel has executed people waving white flags have been confirmed and amplified by witnesses, international rights organizations, media sources, and even the Israeli military itself."

"On November 17th, CNN aired a video taken on a street in Gaza showing a man, Abu Ahmad, carrying a white flag and sitting in shock next to his son, who was shot in the head and killed by Israeli soldiers. Abu and his son, waving a white flag, were following Israeli instructions to evacuate towards the south when Israeli soldiers shot and killed Ahmad."

"An eleven-year-old boy in Gaza witnessed his parents being killed by the IDF while they waved white flags. "The Israelis came in and shot my father and mother. My father was carrying a white flag, my mother went to see him, and they shot her too."

"Video evidence shows a Palestinian woman, who was walking with her grandchildren and waving white flags, who was shot by the IDF in Gaza City on November 12th while she and others were following Israel's orders to evacuate."

"On Jan 25, 13-year-old Nahed Barbakh was shot while carrying a white flag in the middle of the street. His brother who rushed to rescue him was also shot and killed."

The Israeli military killed residents and medical personnel in hospitals:

"On November 10th, reports and a video circulated on social media of the Israeli military opening fire on displaced residents and medical personnel who were trying to evacuate the besieged Annasir Children's Hospital. One of the videos shows many people walking out of the gates of the hospital complex, waving white flags. Suddenly, shots are fired toward the residents and medical crews, and they are forced to return to the besieged hospital."

"Arab TV (@AlarabyTV on Twitter) shared the testimony of Doctor Khaled Abu Samra, who worked at Al Shifa Hospital. In his testimony, he shared that a family trying to leave the hospital complex while raising a white flag was killed by Israeli soldiers."

"On December 22, Al-Jazeera reported that Israeli forces shot and then bulldozed over pregnant women in labor. The women were waving white flags and trying to reach a hospital when they were killed."

The Israeli military killed Israeli hostages:

"On December 16, 2023, the Israeli military released a statement reporting that Israeli soldiers shot and killed three Israeli hostages in Gaza who were waving white flags. [...] Two of the Israeli hostages were immediately killed by the Israeli soldier, while the third hid in a nearby building. As IDF soldiers approached the building where the third hostage was hiding, they heard shouts in Hebrew asking for help. The IDF soldiers entered the building and killed the hostage."

Israel has a history of white-flag executions:

"In 2009, Human Rights Watch investigated and verified Israel's targeting of civilians in Gaza who were waving white flags. During Israel's December 2008-January 2009 assault on Gaza, the Israeli military killed eleven and injured at least eight civilians who were waving white flags. Additionally, no Palestinian fighters were near the civilians whom Israeli forces targeted. [...] The civilian victims were in plain view and posed no apparent security threat."

"In 2014, an international independent fact-finding mission found that in July 2014, Israeli forces opened fire on civilians - carrying white flags - attempting to evacuate Khuzaa village, which Israeli forces had been besieging for several days."

Israel Bombed a School

According to the UN human rights office, Israel bombed a school inside a refugee camp in 2023.

"The [Israeli army] strike against Al Ahli Arab Hospital is an atrocity. We are equally outraged by the deadly strike on the same day on an UNRWA school located in Al Maghazi refugee camp that sheltered some 4000 displaced people, as well as two densely populated refugee camps," a group of UN experts said.[34]

Israel Blockaded, Starved, and Killed Palestinians

In 2023, Israel began a siege blockade against Gaza. In early 2024, Israeli troops killed hundreds of Palestinians waiting for food in a besieged, famine situation. Al Jazeera writes[35]:

"More than 100 Palestinians have been killed and some 700 others wounded after Israeli troops opened fire on hundreds waiting for food aid southwest of Gaza City, health officials say, as the besieged enclave faces an unprecedented hunger crisis.

"People had congregated at al-Rashid Street, where aid trucks carrying flour were believed to be on the way. Al Jazeera verified footage showing the bodies of dozens of killed and wounded Palestinians being carried onto trucks as no ambulances could reach the area.

"Reporting from the scene, Al Jazeera's Ismail al-Ghoul said that after opening fire, Israeli tanks advanced and ran over many of the dead and injured bodies. "It is a massacre, on top of the starvation threatening citizens in Gaza," he said."

Earlier, in 2023, A panel of UN experts on human rights made the following statements about the situation in Palestine[36]:

"The [panel of UN] experts raised serious humanitarian and legal concerns over Israel tightening its 16-year siege of the enclave and its population and long-standing occupation, depriving 2.2 million people of essential food, fuel, water, electricity and medicine. An estimated 50,000 pregnant women in Gaza, are in desperate need of prenatal and postnatal care. The number of internally displaced people across the Gaza Strip is estimated at around one million."

"The complete siege of Gaza coupled with unfeasible evacuation orders and forcible population transfers, is a violation of international humanitarian and criminal law. It is also unspeakably cruel."

"They recalled that the UN Security Council has repeatedly condemned the use of starvation of civilians as a method of warfare, which is prohibited under international humanitarian and criminal law. The unlawful denial of humanitarian access and depriving civilians of objects indispensable to their survival are also a violation of international humanitarian law, the experts warned."

Israeli Army Repeatedly Bombed Civilian Buildings

According to the Middle East Eye, Israel repeatedly bombed several civilian buildings in Gaza in 2023. B'Tselem and Al Jazeera reported similar (higher) statistics. They made the following statements:

"Israel is carrying out a widespread, systematic bombing campaign of Gaza's civilian infrastructure."[37]

"Israeli air force dropped some 2,000 munitions and more than 1,000 tonnes of bombs on Gaza, the army said, having shelled 20 high-rise residential buildings, mosques, hospitals, banks and other civilian infrastructure."[38]

"At least 10 mosques have been demolished in Israel's bombardment of Gaza so far, according to the Islamic affairs ministry in the enclave."[39]

"Palestine's Ministry of Islamic Affairs in Gaza announced on Monday that Israeli bombing destroyed the headquarters of the Holy Quran radio station."[40]

"The Islamic National Bank of Gaza was bombed during live television coverage of Israel's bombardment."[41]

"A year after it was last bombed, the Palestine Tower, a 14-storey residential building in the middle of Gaza City with panoramic views, has been flattened. Survivors told Middle East Eye that they had saved and borrowed thousands of dollars to rebuild their homes after Israel's last bombing."[42]

This aligns with previous actions taken by Israel. For example, in 2014, Amnesty International wrote: "[Israel destroyed] four multistorey buildings [...] in contravention of international humanitarian law."[43]

"Both the facts on the ground and statements made by Israeli military spokespeople at the time indicate that the attacks were a collective punishment against the people of Gaza and were designed to destroy their already precarious livelihoods."[44]

"Even if the Israeli authorities had good reason to believe that a part of a building was being used for military purposes, they had an obligation to choose means and methods of attack that would minimize harm to civilians and their property," says Philip Luther. "The Israeli army have previously conducted air strikes on specific apartments in high-rise buildings without their complete destruction."[45]

Israeli is Collectively Punishing and Killing All Palestinians

Despite Israeli politicians and leaders portraying the events starting in October 2023 as self-defense, Israeli forces indiscriminately killed Palestinians.

According to The Prospect[46]:

"Richard Goldstone, a distinguished South African judge who happened to be both a Jew and a Zionist, [headed an investigation] by an independent fact-finding mission appointed by the UN Human Rights Council.

"The Goldstone team investigated 36 incidents involving the IDF. It found:

- "11 incidents in which Israeli soldiers launched direct attacks against civilians with lethal outcomes (in only one cause was there a possible "justifiable military objective")

- Seven incidents where civilians were shot leaving their homes "waving white flags and, in some of the cases, following an injunction from the Israeli forces to do so"

- "An attack, executed "directly and intentionally" on a hospital

- "Numerous incidents where ambulances were prevented from attending to the severely injured

- "Several attacks on civilian infrastructure with no military significance, such as flour mills, chicken farms, sewage works and water wells—all part of a campaign to deprive civilians of basic necessities.

"In the words of the report, much of this extensive damage was "not justified by military necessity and carried out unlawfully and wantonly.

"[...] While the Israeli government sought to portray its operations as essentially a response to rocket attacks in the exercise of the right to self-defence, "the [Goldstone] Mission itself considers the plan to have been directed, at least in part, at a different target: the people of Gaza as a whole."

Israeli Army Bombed Several Palestinian Hospitals

As of March 2024, Wikipedia lists several hospitals that the Israeli army attacked and/or destroyed[47]. These include:

- The Turkish-Palestinian Friendship Hospital (October 30, 2023)

- The Diagnostic Cancer Treatment Centre of the Al-Ahli Arab Hospital (October 14, 2023)

- Al-Quds hospital

- Indonesia hospital

- The entrance of the Al-Nasser Children's Hospital

- Al-Rantisi Hospital

- Al-Awda Hospital (November 22, 2023)

- Khan Younis' field hospital

- Al-Shifa Hospital (March 18, 2024)[48]

Israel's military specifically targeted Al-Shifa hospital in Gaza City "with tanks and heavy gunfire, resulting in deaths and injuries, Palestinian officials have said [...] Gaza's Ministry of Health said about 30,000 people, including displaced civilians, wounded patients and medical staff are trapped inside the complex."[49]

"Gaza's media office says more than 400 people – patients, war-displaced and healthcare staff – have been killed during Israel's 13-day attack on the al-Shifa Hospital."[50]

As of January 18, 2024, none of Gaza's hospitals remain fully functional.[51]

Middle East Eye, Al Jazeera, and B'Tselem also note that several hospitals have been attacked, destroyed, or disabled.

"Numerous hospitals and medical centres have been attacked."[52]

"Palestine's health ministry announced that the children's section of the Shifa hospital complex had been damaged by Israel's bombing and that the shelling had caused parts of the ceiling to collapse and fall."[53]

"The Beit Hanoun Hospital had been rendered out of service due to constant Israeli bombing in close proximity to the building."[54]

"Medecins Sans Frontieres (MSF), the humanitarian organisation also known as Doctors Without Borders, said that Israeli forces struck Gaza's Indonesian hospital, as well as an ambulance in front of the Nasser Hospital in southern Gaza."[55]

According to the UN human rights office, in 2023, Israel issued two warnings that an airstrike was imminent unless the Al Ahli Arab Hospital in Gaza City was evacuated. They bombed it, and killed 470 civilians.[56] This is contrary to the Israeli narrative that Hamas bombed their own hospital.

"The [Israeli army] strike against Al Ahli Arab Hospital is an atrocity. We are equally outraged by the deadly strike on the same day on an UNRWA school located in Al Maghazi refugee camp that sheltered some 4000 displaced people, as well as two densely populated refugee camps," a group of UN experts said.[57]

The World Health Organization (WHO) documented more than 136 attacks on health care services in the occupied Palestinian territory, including 59 attacks on the Gaza Strip, which resulted in the death of at least 16 health workers, between October 7th and 20th.[58]

Justice for All states even more alarming statistics[59]:

- Israeli troops damaged or destroyed 28 hospitals and 64 healthcare facilities

- At least 756 health workers have been killed or injured

- 163 ambulances have been damaged

Israel Bombed Refugee Camps Multiple Times

In October 2023, Israel bombed the Al Maghazi refugee camp, targeting a school inside the camp[60]. Later in November, they bombed the refugee camp again. Time Magazine writes:

"Israeli warplanes struck a refugee camp in the Gaza Strip early Sunday, killing at least 40 people and wounding dozens. [...] Airstrikes hit the Maghazi refugee camp in central Gaza overnight, killing at least 40 people and wounding 34 others, the Health Ministry said."[61]

Israel Illegally Used Phosphorus Bombs

According to Human Rights Watch and Amnesty International, a number of photos and video evidence confirm that Israel illegally used white phosphorus bombs against Palestinians in 2023 [62] [63], which are prohibited under the U.N. convention on weapons.[64]

White Phosphorus bombs can burn through metal and bone, can "burn down houses and cause egregious harm to civilians"[65], especially when airburst in densely-populated urban areas.[66] [67]

"Any time that white phosphorus is used in crowded civilian areas, it poses a high risk of excruciating burns and lifelong suffering."[68]

Human Rights Watch published a report on Israel's extensive use of white phosphorus from December 27, 2008, to January 18, 2009.[69]

Israel Bombed Gaza's Oldest Church

According to Al Jazeera, at least 18 people died after Israel bombed Gaza's oldest church, the Saint Porphyrius Church in Gaza City[70]:

"The Greek Orthodox church – the oldest in the city, located in the Zaytoun neighbourhood – has traditionally served as a sanctuary for both Christians and Muslims during Israel's periodic wars against Gaza.

"The church was sheltering hundreds of people when an Israeli bomb severely damaged one of the four buildings in its compound on Thursday evening, causing its ceiling to collapse and leaving dozens trapped under slabs of concrete, according to witnesses.

"By Friday afternoon, the Orthodox Patriarchate of Jerusalem told Al Jazeera at least 18 people were confirmed to have been killed, including several children.

"About 200 children, women, elderly and sick people were taking shelter at the church when Israeli warplanes targeted the building with two raids."[71]

Israel Bombed Food Distribution Centers

In March 2024, during a human rights catastrophe and hunger crisis in Palestine, Israel bombed an UNRWA food distribution center - one of the few left in Rafah.[72] Tasnim News Agency, Al Arabiya, and The Hill report:

"[...] the strike hit one of the very few remaining UNRWA distribution centers in the eastern part of Rafah. "Today's attack on one of the very few remaining UNRWA distribution centers in the Gaza Strip comes as food supplies are running out, hunger is widespread and, in some areas, turning into famine," Lazzarini said."[73]

"Israel's military struck a United Nations food distribution center in the Gaza Strip on Tuesday, killing a staff member and at least four other people, according to the U.N. and Gaza health officials.

"Over five months of war in Gaza, Israel has hit more than 150 facilities belonging to the main U.N. aid provider for Palestinians, UNRWA, according to the agency. A quarter of Gaza's population is starving, the United Nations has warned."[74]

Israel's Systemic Torture of Palestinians

According to Wikipedia: "According to Lisa Hajjar (2005) and Dr. Rachel Stroumsa, the director of the Public Committee Against Torture in Israel, torture has been an abiding characteristic of Israeli methods of interrogation of Palestinians. [...] Reports of torture as a means of extracting confessions arguably began early in the occupation, on evidence for the first decade."[75]

Reports on methods of torture include[76]:

- Stripping prisoners naked

- Subjecting them to cold showers and cold

- Hanging prisoners from meat hooks

- Daily beatings with fists and sticks

- Alternate immersions of the victim in hot and cold water

- Beating of genitals

- Applying electrical devices to prisoners

- Applying high frequency sonic noise to prisoners

- Refrigeration

- Prolonged hanging by the hands or feet

- Inserting objects into their private parts

- Being smeared with vomit or urine

- Being confined in a "coffin"

- Suspension by the wrists

- Denial of food, water, and access to toilets

- Being threatened to have their sisters, wives or mothers raped

According to a communication by the International Federation for Human Rights and the Public Committee Against Torture in Israel (PCATI): "Over 1300 complaints of torture by Israeli authorities were submitted to Israel's Justice Ministry between 2001 and June 2021. These have resulted in two criminal investigations and no indictments."[77]

"The methods used during [...] interrogations include methods explicitly prohibited by the Israeli High Court of Justice since 1999 [...]. These include shackling detainees to chairs in various stress positions, e.g., the so-called 'banana' and 'frog' positions, sometimes while shaking, slapping or beating them, or pulling limbs in unnatural directions. Sleep deprivation is particularly common, sometimes by multiple prolonged interrogations each lasting over 30 hours, as well as interrogation or accommodation in extremely cold temperatures, and detention in filthy, insect- infested cells, with constant artificial lighting. PCATI has documented cases of nude interrogation; denying access to toilets; and sexual intimidation, as well as threats to family members. These different methods are often used simultaneously or in cyclical repetition, over a period of several days. PCATI received testimony from detainees who said that they had provided false confessions in the hope of putting an end to interrogations."[78]

78-80% of a sample of detainees in 1985 said they had been sexually molested.[79]

The Israeli Military Desecrated Cemeteries

CNN writes:[80] "[In 2023] the Israeli military has desecrated at least 16 cemeteries in its ground offensive in Gaza, a CNN investigation has found, leaving gravestones ruined, soil upturned, and, in some cases, bodies unearthed. [...]

"CNN has reviewed satellite imagery and social media footage showing the destruction of cemeteries and witnessed it firsthand while traveling with the IDF in a convoy. Together the evidence reveals a systemic practice where Israeli ground forces have advanced across the Gaza Strip."

Israel Forced Eviction and Demolition

In 2021, Israel forced eviction and demolition in the town of Sheikh Jarrah, which is a predominantly Palestinian neighbourhood in East Jerusalem.

"The UN's human rights office called on Israel to immediately halt all forced evictions, including those in the Sheikh Jarrah neighborhood of East Jerusalem."[81] The eviction violates Israel's obligations under international law.[82]

Israel forced eviction of Palestinians, and confiscated private property, which is illegal under international law [3], in violation of the Geneva Convention [83], and a "prima facie war crime."[84]

Israeli Aircraft Destroyed Palestinian Crops, Farms

―――――

Yeni Safak reports[85], in 2024, that "the Palestinian Agricultural Work Committees Union has accused Israel of intentionally using chemicals like white phosphorus on farmlands in the Gaza Strip, resulting in soil contamination and potential cancer risks for agricultural workers. [...]

"These attacks result in the accumulation of carcinogenic substances in the soil, posing a risk of cancer for those who would work on these lands in the future.

"He emphasized that Israel's systematic chemical attacks on usable agricultural lands have caused Palestinians to develop respiratory diseases and skin cancer due to the chemicals used."

In other article, they mention that "Israel used many internationally banned munitions in the Gaza Strip, such as white phosphorus, harmful bombs, and missiles [...] [and] these weapons could cause blindness, cancer, as well as amputation of hands and feet, and skin burns in the future."[86]

Elsewhere, B'Tselem, Al Mezan Center for Human Rights, Euromed Rights, and The Guardian report that on several occasions, from as early as 2013,[87] Israeli crop-dusters sprayed "unknown" herbicides into Palestinian lands and farmlands, without prior notification or warning.[88]

According to Al Mezan, "the Israeli military's aerial spraying of herbicides constitutes a violation of both Israeli constitutional and administrative law, as well as of international humanitarian and human rights laws."[89]

The effects of spraying on Palestinians included asthma, loss of consciousness, rash; resulted in the death of hundreds of animals[90]; caused leaf blight, lost crops, and the destruction of arable land[91]; and ultimately caused "unpredictable and uncontrollable damage."[92]

In 2015, aerial spraying of herbicides destroyed or damaged 187 hectares of crops. The Ecologist writes: "The spraying has had a devastating effect on the farmers by imposing on them total or near total loss of farm income, leaving many of them deep in debt for the cost of agricultural inputs."[93]

As well as suffering the immediate loss of crops and income, some of the farmers may now be forced out of agriculture altogether, unwilling to repeat the risk of losing their crops again."[94]

While Israel ostensibly sprayed in the "buffer zone" between Israel and Gaza, sprays reached as far as 700 meters away.[95]

The buffer zone itself covers roughly 35% of Gaza's arable land, making agriculture a risky activity for Palestinians[96] who are already facing a blockade of food (in 2023).

Israel Poured Concrete into Palestinian Wells

In a long and thorough article, Snopes published details about Israelis pouring concrete into two Palestinian wells.[97]

The video shows "Israeli settlers and army [pouring] cement into two water holes" in July, 2023.

Al Jazeera English published the video, with the caption: "Video footage shows Israeli army personnel pouring cement into a water source which supplies Palestinians near the city of Hebron in the occupied West Bank."

In August 2023, B'tselem published "additional footage of the incident from a different angle" on YouTube, with the title "Israel pours concrete into well and destroys irrigation system in the Palestinian village of al-Hijrah, south of Hebron" and this caption: "On Wednesday morning, 26 July 2023, Civil Administration personnel arrived with a military and Border Police escort, a bulldozer and a cement mixer at the Palestinian village of al-Hijrah, south of Hebron. The forces poured concrete into four water wells and destroyed a roughly 20-meter-long pipe used to irrigate crops, damaging the crops themselves along the way."[98]

Israel Cut Off Electricity Despite an Energy Crisis

Palestine, and Gaza in particular, face an energy crisis. Wikipedia describes it as "an ongoing and growing electricity crisis faced by nearly two million residents of the Gaza Strip, with regular power supply being provided only for a few hours a day on a rolling blackout schedule."[99]

Palestine largely depends on the Israeli Energy Company for electricity. Wikipedia states that "Palestine produces no oil or natural gas and is predominantly dependent on the Israel Electric Corporation (IEC) for electricity."[100] Additionally, "almost all of liquid fuel used in the Palestinian territories is supplied by or via Israel."[101]

Human Rights Watch says[102] "international humanitarian law requires Israel, as the occupying power in Gaza, to ensure that the basic needs of the civilian population are provided for," and calls deprivation of electricity "a war crime." They also say "It is cruel and contrary to international law."

Israel cut electricity to Palestine on several occasions:

- In 2015: Wikipedia states: "On 23 February 2015, [the Israeli Energy Company] intentionally cut off the West Bank power for about 45 minutes due to unpaid bills. Two days later it again cut off power, stating it was a warning to the PA to begin paying down the debt, which at that time was NIS 1.9 billion."[103]

- In 2016: Wikipedia writes: "On 31 March 2016, IEC again cut power to parts of the West Bank, in the Jericho area, because of the NIS 1.7 billion debt. On 4 April, IEC cut power in the Bethlehem area, and the following day it cut power in the Hebron area."[104]

• In 2021: Human Rights Watch writes: "During the first nine months of 2021, families in Gaza on average had to make do without centrally provided electricity for more than 11 hours a day, according to OCHA."[105]

• In 2023: "Al Jazeera writes: "Israel cut off the electricity supply and blocked the entry of food and fuel to the Gaza Strip as part of a 'total siege' strategy."[106]

Israel Blacked Out Internet in Gaza, then Attacked

In October 2023, as a result of heavy Israeli ground strikes,[107] Palestinians experienced a total communication blackout:

"Palestinians are experiencing a total communication blackout in Gaza, according to civil society groups and journalists on the ground."[108]

The blackout affected internet, cellular and landline services.[109] This also affected the Palestine Red Crescent emergency medical services in the area, "due to the Israeli authorities cutting off all landline, cellular and internet communications."[110]

The Telegraph writes[111]:

"The Israeli military has defended the complete telecommunications blackout on the Gaza Strip, saying that it will do whatever it has to do to protect its forces.

"The entire of the Gaza Strip was knocked offline on Friday night before Israel extended its ground incursion into the north of the besieged enclave.

"Asked whether Israel had knocked out cellular services at the start of the ground offensive that began on Friday night, Rear Admiral Daniel Hagari said: 'We do what we have to do to secure our forces for as long as we must, temporary or permanent, as much as we need to and we will not say anything further about that.'"

Israel Killed Journalists

Justice For All notes that "Over 130 journalists and media workers have been killed in Gaza, and many injured.[112] [...] More than 173 media offices in Gaza have been completely or partially destroyed by Israeli attacks."[113]

According to the Committee to Protect Journalists (CPJ), in October 2023 alone[114]:

- 95 journalists were confirmed dead: 90 Palestinian, 2 Israeli, and 3 Lebanese

- 16 journalists were reported injured

- 4 journalists were reported missing

- 25 journalists were arrested

Causes of death of the journalists include[115]:

- Killed in Israeli airstrikes in Gaza, along with ten or more family members

- Killed, along with family members, in Israeli missile strikes that targeted their family's house

- Killed in a shelling attack from the direction of Israel near the Lebanon border

- Killed when Israeli warplanes struck an area housing several media outlets

- Shot and killed in Gaza

- Shot and killed at Erez Crossing

- Killed in a Hamas attack on Israel

- Found dead

This is the official count, which is likely an undercount, according to CPJ. In addition, they report:[116]

- 100 additional reports of journalists killed, missing, detained, or threatened

- 48 media facilities in Gaza were hit or destroyed

According to CPJ, the death of Palestinian American journalist Shireen Abu Akleh of Al Jazeera, who was shot and killed wearing a helmet and vest that was labeled as press, "was not a one-off, but rather part of a long, devastating pattern. The organization's report found that at least 20 journalists have been killed by Israeli military fire since 2001 for which 'to date, no one has been held accountable.'"[117]

Israel Killed Foreign Nationals and Escaped Accountability

In April 2024, Israeli military forces killed foreign aid workers from the World Central Kitchen.[118] USA Today writes:

"[IDF] forces had targeted a World Central Kitchen convoy in the Gaza Strip "systematically, car by car," killing seven aid workers.

"Humanitarian experts said the deaths were all the more striking because World Central Kitchen was known among aid groups both for its caution and its close coordination with the Israeli military in delivering aid.

"If World Central Kitchen – run by an internationally respected celebrity chef, boasting a formidable relationship with the Israeli Defense Forces, operating on a "deconflicted" route arranged with the military – can be attacked, observers say, then anyone in Gaza can.

"What this incident shows us is the IDF's total disregard for the protection of civilians in Gaza," former National Security Council spokesman Tommy Vietor said in an interview."

Earlier, in 2003, foreign national Rachel Corrie, along with some others, went to Gaza to protest and try to prevent the destruction of Palestinian homes and wells. Although dressed in an orange vest for visibility, an Israeli army bulldozer ran her over, and she died of her wounds. The Institute for Middle-East Understanding writes[119]:

"On March 16, 2003, dressed in fluorescent orange vests and using a bullhorn to make their presence known to Israeli soldiers, Rachel and a group of seven other American and British ISM volunteers set off to attempt to prevent the destruction of Palestinian homes in the so-called Philadelphi corridor area of Rafah, along the border with Egypt.

"Late in the afternoon, after several hours of confronting soldiers who were using two 60-ton armored Caterpillar D9 weaponized bulldozers to destroy homes, Rachel slipped while standing on a mound of earth in front one of the bulldozers and was run over. Severely injured, she was taken to hospital by ambulance where she was declared dead."

A witness writes: ""The driver cannot have failed to see her. As the blade pushed the pile, the earth rose up. Rachel slid down the pile. It looks as if her foot got caught. The driver didn't slow down; he just ran over her. Then he reversed the bulldozer back over her again."[120]

Israel's Systemic Use of Sexual Assault Against Palestinian Women

In March 2024, Dr Aliya Khan, a clinical professor of medicine and a board member of the Union of Medical Care and Relief Organisations (UOSSM), reports to the Middle East Monitor:[121]

"Women in Gaza are being raped and it is not being investigated or reported," Khan notes. "No one is speaking about this in the Western media. I just received a report from our Canadian medical colleague on the ground in Gaza that the Al-Khayr hospital, which is next to Nasser Hospital, has been attacked.

"The paramedic informed the physician that a woman was raped for two days until she lost her ability to speak. Another woman at the Nasr Hospital was stripped of her clothing by Israeli soldiers in front of her husband and brother, and when one of them took their clothes off to cover her the Israeli soldiers killed both her brother and husband.

"These are credible reports from Canadian physicians serving in Gaza."

As mentioned earlier, 78-80% of a sample of (child) detainees in 1985 said they had been sexually molested.[122]

Israel and Israelis Attacked and Censored Media

In addition to killing journalists, Israel also attacked, arrested, threatened, and censored several journalists. According to CPJ research: "there were more than 10 incidents of assaults, arrests, threats, cyberattacks and censorship targeting journalists as they carry out their work in Israel and in the Palestinian territories of Gaza and the West Bank."[123]

From the 2023 conflict alone, assaults include[124]:

- Journalist Israel Frey "went into hiding after his home was attacked the previous day by a mob of far-right Israelis after he expressed solidarity with Palestinians in Gaza." (Additionally reported by Haaretz and Middle East Eye)

- "[Two] BBC Arabic reporters [...] and their team were dragged from their vehicle, searched, and held at gunpoint by police in the Israeli city of Tel Aviv, despite their vehicle being marked "TV" in red tape and [the journalists] presenting their press cards to police."[125]

- A reporting team of Sky News Arabia "in the southern Israeli city of Ashkelon was assaulted by Israeli police. The channel's correspondent, Firas Lutfi, described how the police pointed rifles at his head, forced him to undress, confiscated their phones, and escorted them out of the area."

In 2021, "two unidentified members of a right-wing Israeli demonstration attacked a Kan News team consisting of reporter Yoav Zehavi and camera operator Rolik Nowitzki, who had been covering the demonstration."[126]

Arrests include:

- Six Palestinian journalists arrested in two separate incidents in 2023.[127]

- The arrest of Hazem Naser, a Palestinian camera operator, in 2021[128]

Cyberattacks include[129]:

- Palestinian Authority's official news agency, Wafa, experienced a cyberattack that disrupted its news website.

- The Jerusalem Post's website being down due to a series of cyberattacks from the previous day. (The group Anonymous Sudan claimed responsibility for these attacks, according to Time magazine.)

In terms of censorship: "On October 16, the IDF ordered the West Bank-based J-Media agency to shut down, according to the Palestinian press freedom group MADA and New Arab. In a statement, IDF described the media outlet as "an illegal organization" and said the closure was necessary for "the sake of the security of the State of Israel and for the safety of the public and public order," those sources said, adding that J-Media complied and ceased its operations immediately. J-Media provides footage and media services to broadcasters and covers Palestinian news, according to press freedom group SKeyes Center for Media and Cultural Freedom and CPJ's review of its website."[130]

Israel Evacuated a Million Palestinians in 24 hours

In October 2023, Amnesty International reported that the Israeli army gave Palestinians in Gaza 24 hours notice to evacuate from Gaza and Gaza City to the south of the Gaza Strip "for their safety and protection" before they started bombing it. The Israeli army themselves admitted the impossibility of this order, which resulted in panic and a mass forced displacement of more than 1.1 million Palestinian Muslims.[131]

Israel Illegally Seized Land

As recently as March 22, 2004, Israel "declared 800 hectares (1977 acres) in the occupied West Bank as [Israeli] state land" according to Al Jazeera.[132]

However, Israeli expropriation of Palestinian land has a long history. According to Wikipedia: "From 1969 to 2019 Israel had issued over 1150 military seizure orders alone.

"According to a 2019 study by Dror Etkes, military seizure orders, based on military and security requirements, have resulted in the expropriation of over 100,000 dunams (25,000 acres) of Palestinian land. 40% of such temporary requisitions have then been turned over to settlements."[133]

According to B'Tselem: "Some half a million Israelis are now living [in] more than 300,000 in 121 settlements and about one hundred outposts, which control 42 percent of the land area of the West Bank [...] The principal means Israel used for this purpose was declaration of "state land," a mechanism that resulted in the seizure of more than 900,000 dunams of land (16% percent of the West Bank), with most of the declarations being made in 1979-1992."[134]

Amnesty International writes: "Since the occupation first began in June 1967, Israel's ruthless policies of land confiscation, illegal settlement and dispossession, coupled with rampant discrimination, have inflicted immense suffering on Palestinians, depriving them of their basic rights."[135]

Israeli Settlements are Illegal Under International Law

Numerous UN resolutions and prevailing international opinion hold that Israeli settlements in the West Bank, East Jerusalem and the Golan Heights are a violation of international law, including UN Security Council resolutions in 1979, 1980, and 2016.[136]

Israeli settlements contribute to serious human rights abuses against Palestinians living in Palestine, including[137]:

- The right to life

- The right to adequate housing

- The right to equality and non-discrimination

- The right to liberty and fair trial

- The right to an effective remedy

- The right to security of person and to health

- The rights of children

- The right to water

- The right to education

- The right to peaceful assembly

- Labour rights

- The right to freedom of movement

Israel Rejected International Calls for Ceasefire

During the conflict of October 2023, 120 out of 184 countries in the UN voted for a ceasefire in Palestine.[138]

Al Jazeera writes: "Israeli Prime Minister Benjamin Netanyahu also dismissed growing calls for a ceasefire, saying that such action would constitute 'surrender to terrorism.'"[139]

"Speaking to reporters on Monday, Israeli Prime Minister Benjamin Netanyahu emphatically rejected calls for a ceasefire, saying that 'this is a time for war.'"[140]

In November of the same year, Israeli warplanes bombed a refugee camp, "despite U.S. appeals for a pause to get aid to desperate civilians."[141]

Israeli Settlers and IDF Damage Olive Trees

The Ecologist writes: "The uprooting and cutting down of over a million olive and fruit trees in occupied Palestine since 1967 [until 2015] is an attack on a symbol of life, and on Palestinian culture and survival [... and] a grave crime under international humantarian law, the arboricide is also contrary to Jewish religious teachings."[142]

"Armed Israelis are systematically wrecking trees that have stood for hundreds of years and frequently provide the only livelihood for Palestinian families."[143]

The destruction of the olive trees is also a specific violation of Article 54 of the 1977 Protocol to the 1949 Geneva Conventions, which prohibits the "starvation of civilians as a method of warfare."[144]

"Since 1967 some 800,000 olive trees have been uprooted by Israeli forces and settlers in the occupied West Bank alone, according to research from the Palestinian Authority and the Applied Research Institute Jerusalem. This has threatened the livelihood of 80,000 families."[145]

"Over 9000 olive trees have been destroyed in the West Bank since August 2020 [alone], according to the International Committee of the Red Cross (ICRC)."[146]

"For years, the ICRC has observed a seasonal peak in violence by Israeli settlers residing in certain settlements and outposts in the West Bank towards Palestinian farmers and their property in the period leading up to the olive harvest season, as well as during the harvest season itself, in October and November."[147]

""Farmers also experience acts of harassment and violence that aim at preventing a successful harvest, not to mention the destruction of farming equipment or the uprooting and burning of olive trees."[148]

55

Israel Protesters Danced and Cheered While Blocking Gaza Aid

Snopes published a lengthy article about a video of Israel protesters dancing to music while blocking aid to Gaza.[149] Highlights from the article include:

- Confirming the video as authentic and unaltered

- A tweet from Dr. Andrewas Krieg: "[Y]ou have people feeling comfortable to organise a rave to block humanitarian aid, to women and children a stone throw away being who are decimated by an indiscriminate war machine."

- A post in Hebrew showing a different angle, with the text: "The Kerem Shalom crossing was blocked for the movement of aid trucks to Hamas. Take a good look at Gaza. We will still dance in your ruin."

The article includes a lengthy citation from the Washington Post:

"With dawn comes a new busload of demonstrators, ultra-Orthodox children and teens from northern Israel. They strap on their tefillin and pray. Some dance. A group with a guitar sing songs about the military. They use the border crossing bathrooms. No one asks them to leave.

"Every explosion in Gaza raises a cheer.

"Dead, dead, dead Arabs," one camper shouts at a roaring volley of outgoing fire. Then she notes the presence of a reporter. "Hamas," she corrects herself."

The same article cites the Washington Post as saying: "the U.N. Office for the Coordination Prof Humanitarian Affairs said it could not provide data on how many trucks had been disrupted at the crossing."

Gaza is the World's Largest Open-Air Prison

According to Human Rights Watch, Gaza is - and has been since 2007 - the largest "open-air" prison in the world. "Israel, with Egypt's help, has turned Gaza into an open-air prison."[150]

"Since 2007, Israeli authorities have, with narrow exceptions, banned Palestinians from leaving through Erez, the passenger crossing from Gaza into Israel, through which they can reach the West Bank and travel abroad via Jordan. Israel also prevents Palestinian authorities from operating an airport or seaport in Gaza. Israeli authorities also sharply restrict the entry and exit of goods."[151]

Slate Magazine writes: "Gaza became a resource-starved and overpopulated open-air prison, forced to rely on Israel for food, water, electricity, trade, mail delivery, access to fishing, medical care, or contact with the outside world. From then on, Israel has effectively treated Hamas as the prisoner organization responsible for preventing the inmates—none of whom have been placed on trial, and all of whom have life sentences—from harming Israel or Israelis."[152]

"This relationship has been enforced by punishing incursions into the strip by the Israeli military [...] [and] in the process, killing more than 6,400 Palestinians between 2008 and September 2023, and inflicting billions of dollars of damage."[153]

Palestinians Can't Leave Palestine

———

Bloomberg News published an article in their Opinion category, explaining why Palsetinians can't just leave Gaza[154].

"It is not unreasonable to wonder why the 2.3 million civilians living in the tiny enclave don't flee to safer ground [...] The short answer to that question is: They can't."[155]

"At 139 square miles, the Gaza Strip is approximately the size of Philadelphia, with a third more people. There is very little open space within the enclave where 2 million people can hunker down and wait for the fighting to end."[156]

"Many Gazans are being forced out of their homes and neighborhoods, but there's nowhere safe for them to go."[157]

"Egypt is solicitous about the problems of Palestinians but doesn't want them on its soil. Cairo is already trotting out its usual excuses of poverty and security: Egypt can't afford to host refugees, and they might cause trouble."[158]

"Other Arab nations offer variations of those lines. Jordan already has too many Palestinians (they make up more than half the population of the kingdom) and too many refugees from other places, such as Syria. Turkey, which is sympathetic to the Palestinian cause, likewise has its hands full of refugees from other parts."[159]

"The Gulf Arab states have plenty of land and no shortage of money; Saudi Arabia is currently spending hundreds of billions of dollars building a city it doesn't really need. Their traditional excuse for not taking in Palestinians is that it would let Israel off the hook."[160]

"The civilians in Gaza can't leave, and it's a tragedy twice over that nobody wants them anyway."[161]

Israel is Committing Apartheid Against Palestinians

———

Agnès Callamard, Amnesty International's Secretary General, writes: "Our report reveals the true extent of Israel's apartheid regime. Whether they live in Gaza, East Jerusalem and the rest of the West Bank, or Israel itself, Palestinians are treated as an inferior racial group and systematically deprived of their rights."[162]

Amnesty International writes: "Palestinians facing the brutality of Israel's repression have been calling for an understanding of Israel's rule as apartheid for over two decades. Over time, a broader international recognition of Israel's treatment of Palestinians as apartheid has begun to take shape."[163]

They define apartheid as "a violation of public international law, a grave violation of internationally protected human rights, and a crime against humanity under international criminal law"[164] and state that "Apartheid can best be understood as a system of prolonged and cruel discriminatory treatment by one racial group of members of another with the intention to control the second racial group."[165]

The United Nations analyzes the situation "through the internationally-understood legal definition of apartheid – the system of institutionalized racial segregation practiced in South Africa prior to its dismantling in the early 1990s."[166]

They state that "Israel [...] conforms to the definition [of apartheid] as a 'political regime which so intentionally and clearly prioritizes fundamental political, legal and social rights to one group over another, within the same geographic unit on the basis of one's racial-national-ethnic identity.'"[167]

They continue that "leading international figures – including former UN Secretary General Ban Ki-Moon, Archbishop Desmond Tutu, South African

Foreign Minister Naledi Pandor, and former Israeli Attorney General Michael Ben-Yair – have also all described Israel's occupation as apartheid."[168]

In October 2023, the Director of the New York office of the UN high commissioner for human rights left his post, citing "genocide" of Palestinian citizens as the reason.[169]

"The director of the New York office of the UN high commissioner for human rights has left his post, protesting that the UN is "failing" in its duty to prevent what he categorizes as genocide of Palestinian civilians in Gaza under Israeli bombardment and citing the US, UK and much of Europe as "wholly complicit in the horrific assault."[170]

"Mokhiber, who was stepping down having reached retirement age, wrote: "Once again we are seeing a genocide unfolding before our eyes and the organization we serve appears powerless to stop it."[171]

Systemic Racism Against Palestinians

Wikipedia contains two pages about racisim in Palestine, which highlight the systemic, government-sponsored, and majority-supported racism against Arab Palestinians.

One page, titled "Anti-Arab Racism," includes a sub-section on Israel; and one page, titled "Racisim in Israel," also discusses the topic. Below are some excerpts from both pages, quoted verbatim.

Racism against Arab citizens of Israel on the part of the Israeli state and some Israeli Jews has been identified by critics in personal attitudes, the media, education, immigration rights, housing segregation, and social life. Nearly all such characterizations have been denied by the state of Israel.[172]

Geography textbooks used in Israeli schools were found to portray Arabs as primitive and backwards, with the Nakba, the destruction of Palestinian society in the 1948 Palestine war, disregarded entirely. History textbooks likewise portrayed the Palestinian population negatively, showing them as primitive and collectively to be an enemy. Contrasted with the portrayal of Jews, who were shown to be heroic and progressive, Israeli textbooks delegitimized Arabs and used negative stereotyping of Arabs nearly uniformly.[173]

In a number of occasions, Israeli Jewish demonstrators and rioters used racist anti-Arab slogans. For example, during the Arab riots in October 2000 events, Israelis counter-rioted in Nazareth and Tel Aviv, throwing stones at Arabs, destroying Arab property, with some chanting "death to Arabs".[174]

According to a 2001 report by Human Rights Watch, Israel's school systems for Arab and Jewish children are separate and have unequal conditions to the disadvantage of the Arab children who make up one-quarter of all students. Israeli law does not prohibit Palestinian Arab parents from enrolling their children in Jewish schools, but in practice, very few Palestinian Arab parents do so.[30][32] The report stated that "Government-run Arab schools are a world apart from government-run Jewish schools. In virtually every respect, Palestinian Arab children get an education inferior to that of Jewish children, and their relatively poor performance in school reflects this.[175]

According to the 2004 U.S. State Department Country Reports on Human Rights Practices for Israel and the Occupied Territories, the Israeli government had done "little to reduce institutional, legal, and societal discrimination against the country's Arab citizens." The 2005 U.S. Department of State report on Israel wrote: "[T]he government generally respected the human rights of its citizens; however, there were problems in some areas, including ... institutional, legal, and societal discrimination against the country's Arab citizens."[176]

In 2004, Yehiel Hazan, a member of the Knesset, described the Arabs as worms: "You find them everywhere like worms, underground as well as above."[177]

According to a 2006 poll conducted by Geocartographia for the Centre for the Struggle Against Racism, 41% of Israelis support Arab-Israeli segregation at entertainment venues, 40% believed "the state needs to support the emigration of Arab citizens", and 63% believed Arabs to be a "security and demographic threat" to Israel. The poll found that more than two thirds would not want to live in the same building as an Arab, 36% believed Arab culture to be inferior, and 18% felt hatred when they heard Arabic spoken.[178]

In 2007, the Association for Civil Rights in Israel reported that anti-Arab views had doubled, and anti-Arab racist incidents had increased by 26%.[110] The report quoted polls that suggested 50% of Jewish Israelis do not believe Arab citizens of Israel should have equal rights, 50% said they wanted the government to encourage Arab emigration from Israel, and 75% of Jewish youths said Arabs were less intelligent and less clean than Jews. The Mossawa Advocacy Center for Arab Citizens in Israel reported a tenfold increase in racist incidents against Arabs in 2008. Jerusalem reported the highest number of incidents. The report blamed Israeli leaders for the violence, saying "These attacks are not the hand of fate, but a direct result of incitement against the Arab citizens of this country by religious, public, and elected officials."[179]

The Association for Civil Rights in Israel (ACRI) published reports documenting racism in Israel, and the 2007 report suggested that anti-Arab racism in the country was increasing. One analysis of the report summarized it thus: "Over two-thirds of Israeli teens believe Arabs to be less intelligent, uncultured and violent. Over a third of Israeli teens fear Arabs all together ... The report becomes even grimmer, citing the ACRI's racism poll, taken in March 2007, in which 50% of Israelis taking part said they would not live in the same building as Arabs, will not befriend, or let their children befriend Arabs and would not let Arabs into their homes." The 2008 report from ACRI says the trend of increasing racism is continuing.[180]

Another 2007 report, by the Center Against Racism, also found hostility against Arabs was on the rise. Among its findings, it reported that 75% of Israeli Jews do not approve of Arabs and Jews sharing apartment buildings; that over half of Jews would not want to have an Arab boss and that marrying an Arab amounts to "national treason"; and that 55% of the sample thought Arabs should be kept separate from Jews in entertainment sites. Half wanted the Israeli government to encourage Israeli Arabs to emigrate. About 40% believed Arab citizens should have their voting rights removed.[181]

A March 2010 poll by Tel Aviv University found that 49.5% of Israeli Jewish high school students believe Israeli Arabs should not be entitled to the same rights as Jews in Israel. 56% believe Arabs should not be eligible to the Knesset, the Israeli parliament.[182]

An October 2010 poll by the Dahaf polling agency found that 36% of Israeli Jews favor eliminating voting rights for non-Jews. In recent polling (2003–2009) between 42% and 56% of Israelis agreed that "Israeli Arabs suffer from discrimination as opposed to Jewish citizens"; 80% of Israeli Arabs agreed with that statement in 2009.[183]

A 2012 poll revealed widespread support among Israeli Jews for discrimination against Israeli Arabs.[184]

A poll in 2012 revealed that racist attitudes are embraced by a large majority of Israelis. 59% of Jews said they wanted Jews to be given preference in admission to public employment, 50% wanted the state to generally treat Jews better than Arabs, and over 40% wanted separate housing for Jews and Arabs. According to the poll, 58% supported the use of the term apartheid to represent Israeli policies against Arabs. The poll also showed that the majority of Israeli Jews would not want voting rights extended to Palestinians if the West Bank were annexed by Israel.[185]

In 2013, Nazareth Illit mayor Shimon Gafsou declared that he would never allow that an Arab school, a mosque, or a church be built in his city, despite the fact that Arabs account for 18 percent of its population.[186]

In 2018, the Association for Civil Rights in Israel published a report about anti-democratic legislation passed in Israel. Their report touches on racism, which "erodes the democratic framework of the country as a whole:

"In the 20th Knesset the Basic Law: Israel – The Nation State of the Jewish People was proposed (P/20/1989) by MK Dichter and Others. [...] The law, which in effect is now part of the constitutional framework of the state of Israel, does not deal with [...] human rights obligations, and, in fact, grossly violates the balance between Israel as a Jewish and democratic state. Not only does this law not guarantee human rights to all of its citizens, but specifically infringes the right to equality, the right to language and culture, and the rights of the minority. [...] The law anchors already- present discrimination and racial segregation in renting and buying real estate, violates the right to language, culture and identity to one fifth of the country's citizens, and includes many discriminatory provisions that open the door to widespread practices of racial discrimination in all spheres of life. There is much concern that a Basic Law of this nature will harm the human rights of all Israeli citizens, as it erodes the democratic framework of the country as a whole."[187]

In 2021, Israel began to distribute COVID-19 vaccines to its own citizens, but not to Palestinians.

According to Physicians for Human Rights:[188]

"As vaccination campaigns against COVID-19 expand and intensify worldwide, we are witnessing clear systemic discrimination and inequity around who receives life-saving vaccines and who does not. Such vaccine inequity is particularly disturbing in the Israeli/Palestinian context, where Israel, the occupying power, has ignored its responsibilities under international law to provide for the health of the population in the territory it occupies."[189]

"Although Israel has been praised for rapidly vaccinating a significant percentage of its citizens, it has failed to fulfill its legal and moral obligations to provide COVID-19 vaccines for Palestinians living under Israeli occupation in the West Bank and Gaza. By early March, Israel had fully vaccinated more than half of its citizens, including Israeli settlers illegally living in the Occupied Palestinian Territory (OPT). Meanwhile, Palestinians living under Israeli control are still, by and large, ineligible to receive these life-saving inoculations – a separate and unequal system that leaves them exposed to infection and death while Israeli citizens develop immunity, amid the worst global health crisis in a century."

The UN Office of Human Rights writes: "UN human rights experts* today called on Israel, the occupying power, to ensure swift and equitable access to COVID-19 vaccines for the Palestinian people under occupation."[190]

Palestinian Children and the Six Grave Violations

In 1999, the United Nations Security Council passed the first resolution on children and armed conflict. They identified and condemned six grave violations affecting children the most in times of war.[191] These are:[192]

- Killing and maiming of children

- Recruitment or use of children as soldiers

- Sexual violence against children

- Abduction of children

- Attacks against schools or hospitals

- Denial of humanitarian access for children

For the period from October 7-23, 2023:[193]

Killing and Maiming:

- At least 3038 Palestinian children were killed

- Over 6000 were injured

Attacks on Schools and Hospitals: the World Health Organization (WHO) documented at least 76 attacks on health care, including:

- 20 hospitals damaged

- 24 ambulances damaged

- At least 16 health care workers killed

- At least 30 health care workers injured

- 12 out of 35 hospitals in Gaza are no longer operational

- At least 219 educational facilities (schools) have been damaged

Denial of Humanitarian Access:

- An estimated 1.4 million Palestinians in Gaza are displaced

- Gaza experienced a full electricity blackout after Israeli authorities cut the electricity and fuel supply on October 7 (20 days and counting)

- At least 45 percent of all housing units in the Gaza Strip have been damaged or completely destroyed

- Israel cut off food, water, electricity and fuel from Gaza

Many of these points are independently reported on, and expanded upon, in other sections.

A Leaked Document from the Israeli Ministry of Intelligence

According to WikiLeaks, an organization that "publishes documents of political or historical importance that are censored or otherwise suppressed", a "Verified document from Israeli Ministry of Intelligence on October 13, 2023, suggests forced displacement of Gaza civilians to Egypt would "yield positive and long term strategic results.""[194]

The original document is online as of writing.[195] The document recommends that Israel:[196]

- "Carry out a full transfer of all residents of the Gaza Strip to North Sinai, as the preferred option among the three alternatives it offers regarding the future of the Palestinians in the [Gaza] Strip"

- "Evacuate the Gazan population to Sinai during the war"

- "Establish tent cities and new cities in northern Sinai, which will accommodate the deported population"

- "Create a sterile zone of several kilometers inside Egypt and not allow the population to return to activity or residence near the Israeli border."

Although "the existence of the document does not necessarily indicate that its recommendations are being considered by the security system," the document "features the logo of the Ministry of Intelligence headed by minister Gila Gamliel of the Likud. An official at the Ministry of Intelligence confirmed to "Local Talk" that this is an authentic document, which was distributed to the security system on behalf of the Ministry's Policy Division, and "was not supposed to reach the media."[197]

"The document unequivocally and explicitly recommends carrying out a transfer of civilians from Gaza as the desired outcome of the war."[198]

Statistics on Incarceration of Palestinians

In the West Bank, in 2021, "Israel held 4,460 Palestinians in custody for "security" offenses, including 200 children, many for throwing stones, and 492 in administrative detention without formal charges or trial and based on secret evidence, according to figures by the Israeli human rights group HaMoked and Palestinian prisoner rights group Adameer."[199]

"More than 1,300 complaints of torture, including of painful shackling, sleep deprivation and exposure to extreme temperatures, have been filed with Israel's Justice Ministry since 2001, resulting in two criminal investigations and no indictments, according to the Israeli rights group Public Committee Against Torture."[200]

According to B'Tselem, as of June 2023, the Israel Prison Service (IPS):

- Held 4499 Palestinians in detention or in prison on what it defined as "security" grounds, including 183 from the Gaza Strip.[201]

- Held 147 Palestinian minors in detention or in prison on what it defined "security" grounds.[202]

- Held 1117 Palestinians in administrative detention.[203]

Statistics on Israeli Settlements

Amnesty International provided several statements and statistics around Israeli settlements, spanning from 1967 to 2021:

"Since its occupation in 1967 [until 2019], Israel promoted the creation and expansion of settlements in Palestine, which resulted in:[204]

- "the appropriation of 200,000+ hectares of Palestinian land;

- "the establishment of 250+ settlements, populated by 600,000+ Israeli settlers;

- "the physical enclosure and segregation of the 3 million West Bank Palestinians;

- "the extension of Israeli laws to the West Bank and the creation of a discriminatory legal regime;

"the unequal access to natural resources, social services, property and land for Palestinians in the occupied West Bank."

According to Human Rights Watch's 2022 World Report[205], which covers events that transpired in 2021:

- The Israel government issued tenders for more than 4000 new settlements in Gaza

- 2400 Palestinian house units were made uninhabitable in Gaza

- 55,000 Palestinian house units were damaged in Gaza

- Caused property damage in 287 incidents in West Bank

Quotes from Notable Political Figures of Israel

———

Given the history of human rights violations in Palestine, as well as the vast disparity between Palestinian and Israeli forces, we should ask ourselves why this conflict shows no signs of slowing down, even after 75+ years.

The following quotes, listed chronologically, are from notable figures of Israel, spanning from 1948 to present. To paraphrase PALCIT, "their authors are most often people who have played a direct and important role of political power. This [...] is intended to give a raw material to understand the ideology that has guided the decisions taken since the birth of Zionism to lead to today's Israel."[206]

Many of these quotes come from PALCIT. "[Quotes] (in PALCIT) come either from recognized historians or from media that have shed light on the news. [...] The authenticity of the quotations and their sources have been carefully verified."[207] All PALCIT points reference their primary source, which I have also listed below, along with any additional sources.

An oft-quoted source is an article[208] by David Ben Gurion, one of the founders of Israel, which is quoted below as ibid DBG."

Some recent quotes come directly from their authors' social media accounts.

"When adult males were discovered hiding...-they were killed" (describing how members of several kibbutzes killed the unarmed peasants of Abu Zureiq without a second thought. No investigation was ever decided upon and the number of Palestinians massacred remains unknown.) (April 14, 1948) [209] [210]

"As April began, our War of Independence swung decisively from defense to attack." (David Ben Gurion, April 20, 1954)[211] [212]

"Save your souls, all ye faithful: The Jews are using poison gas and atomic weapons" (Leo Heiman, May 1964). A Zionist officer who fought in 1948, describing some of the methods used to drive out an unarmed population.[213]

"Achieve total victory, the territorial fulfillment of the Land Of Israel." (Yigal Allon, 1966)[214] [215]

"Not one single place built ... that did not have a former Arab population" (Moshe Dayan, April 4, 1969)[216] [217]

"There was no such thing as Palestinians, they never existed." (Golda Maier, June 15, 1969)[218]

"For me the supreme morality is the the jewish people has a right to exist." (Golda Meir, 1969) [219] [220]

"The thesis that the danger of genocide was hanging over us in June 1967, and that Israel was fighting for its physical existence is only bluff; [it] was born and developed after the war." (Israeli Gen. Matityahu Peled, Ha'aretz, March 19, 1972.) [221] [222]

"It is the duty of Israeli leaders to explain to public opinion, clearly and courageously, a certain number of facts that are forgotten with time. The first of these is that there is no Zionism, colonialization or Jewish State without the eviction of the Arabs and the expropriation of their lands." (Yoram Bar Porath, Yediot Aahronot of July 14, 1972.)[223] [224] [225]

"We walked outside, Ben-Gurion accompanying us. Allon repeated his question, 'What is to be done with the Palestinian population?' Ben-Gurion waved his hand in a gesture which said 'Drive them out!'" (Yitzhak Rabin, leaked censored version of Rabin memoirs, published in the New York Times, Oct. 23, 1979)[226] [227] [228]

"All the Arabs are the same. They should all be finished off." (Golda Meir1980)[229] [230]

"Israel wantonly inflicting every possible measure of death" (Former Israeli ambassador to the UN and Minister of Foreign Affairs, Eban outbids Menachem Begin in qualifying Israel's genocidal acts.) (June 16, 1981)[231] [232]

"The Palestinians are beasts walking on two legs." (Menahim Begin, in a speech to the Knesset, quoted by Amnon Kapeliouk, in "Begin and the Beasts" (New Statesman, June 25 1982.) [233] [234]

"To gain control of the area allotted to the Jewish State and ... blocs ... outside those borders" (Indicates that the Dalet Plan (1948) was already aimed at 'controlling' the Palestinian territories beyond the space allocated for a 'Jewish state' in 1947.) (Quotation from the UN / ONU, 1990)[235] [236]

"There was no choice but to kill them. This is not such a big deal" (former Israeli Brigadier General, talking about the massacres of the 1956 Sinai War.) (Arieh Biro, August 21, 1995)[237] [238]

"Drop by drop tactic in which one or two houses are demolished daily" (Edward Said, July 23, 1998)[239] [240]

"Everybody has to move, run and grab as many hilltops as they can to enlarge the settlements because everything we take now will stay ours... Everything we don't grab will go to them." (Ariel Sharon, addressing, as foreign minister, a meeting of militants from the extreme right-wing Tsomet Party (Agence France Presse, Nov. 15, 1998))[241]

"Everything that's grabbed will be in our hands" (Ariel Sharon, November 15, 1998)[242] [243]

"No one has the right to put the Jewish people and the State of Israel on trial." (Ariel Sharon, March 25, 2001)[244] [245]

"They have been ready to make peace with us; it is we who are unwilling." (Yitzhak Frankenthal, July 27, 2002)[246] [247]

"We had to destroy them, otherwise we would have had Arabs here" (Yitzhak Pundak, May 21, 2004)[248] [249]

"We will have to kill them all." (Efraim Eitam, May 24, 2004)[250] [251]

"Commanders and soldiers are safe from tribunals." (Ehud Olmert, January 25, 2009)[252] [253]

"A national duty to prevent the spread of a population that ... does not love Israel." (Ariel Atias, July 2, 2009)[254] [255]

"There is a reason to kill babies." (Yitzhak Shapira, November 9, 2009)[256] [257]

"We must blow Gaza back to the Middle Ages." (Eli Yishai, November 17, 2012)[258] [259]

"I've killed lots of Arabs in my life – and there's no problem with that?" (Moshe Feiglin July 21, 2013)[260] [261]

"What's so horrifying about understanding that the entire Palestinian people is the enemy" (Uri Elitzur, June 30, 2014)[262]

"The entire Palestinian people are the enemy, including its elderly and its women." (Ayelet Shaked, July 1, 2014)[263] [264]

"Gaza will become part of sovereign Israel" (Moshe Feiglin, July 15, 2014)[265] [266]

"Those who are against us ...we need to pick up an ax and cut off his head." (Talking about Palestinians "citizens" of Israel, during an election rally.) (Avigdor Lieberman, March 8, 2015)[267] [268]

"Maintain a Jewish majority even at the price of violation of rights" (Ayelet Shaked, February 13, 2018)[269] [270]

"There is no such thing as a Palestinian nation. There is no Palestinian history. There is no Palestinian language." (Bezalel Smotrich, March 20, 2023)[271]

"Right now, one goal: Nakba! A Nakba that will overshadow the Nakba of 1948." (Ariel Kallner, October 7, 2023)[272]

"I have ordered a complete siege on the Gaza Strip. There will be no electricity, no food, no fuel, everything is closed. We are fighting human animals and we are acting accordingly." (Yoav Gallant, October 9, 2023)[273]

"Jericho Missile! [...] Doomsday weapon! This is my opinion."[274] "Only an explosion that shakes the Middle East will restore this country's dignity, strength and security! It's time to kiss doomsday. Shooting powerful missiles without limit. Not flattening a neighborhood. Crushing and flattening Gaza. Otherwise we did nothing. Not with passwords, with penetrating bombs. without mercy! without mercy!" (Tally Gotliv, October 9, 2023)[275]

"Human animals must be treated as such. There will be no electricity and no water [in Gaza], there will only be destruction. You wanted hell, you will get hell." (Ghassan Ali, October 9, 2023)[276] [277]

"We will turn [Gaza] into an island of ruins." (Benjamin Netanyahu, October 9, 2023)[278]

"It's an entire nation out there that is responsible. This rhetoric about civilians not aware, not involved, it's absolutely not true." (Yitzhak Herzog, October 16, 2023)[279]

"Be triumphant and finish them off and don't leave anyone behind. Erase the memory of them. Erase them, their families, mothers and children. These animals can no longer live. Every Jew with a weapon should go out and kill them. If you have an Arab neighbour, don't wait, go to his home and shoot him." (Ezra Yachin, October 14, 2023)[280]

"There is one and only one solution, which is to completely destroy Gaza before in-vading it, and when I talk about destruction, I mean destruction like it was in Dres-den and Hiroshima, without a nuclear weapon." (Moshe Feiglin, Knesset member)[281]

[In response to being asked about the collective punishment of Palestinian people and Israel's blockade of Gaza] "I am very puzzled by the constant concern which the world is showing for the Palestinian people and is actually showing for these horrible inhuman animals who have done the worst atrocities that this century has seen." (Dan Gillerman, former Israeli ambassador to the UN, October 2023)[282]

"And the children in Gaza – the children in Gaza have brought this upon themselves!" (Merav Ben Ari, Knesset member)[283]

How to Help

The facts and statements above contextualize and highlight the human rights violations, war crimes, and crises in Palestine, Gaza, and the West Bank; both in light of recent events, and historical events that stretch back to 1948. They also illuminate some of the attitudes and beliefs that lead to the ongoing apartheid.

On an individual level, you can make a change to stop the killing. For reference, see: "How You Can Help Stop Israel's Carnage In Gaza - And Support Palestinian Liberation[1]" on YouTube.

Actions outlined in the video, and additional actions, include working collectively as individuals and organizations to:

- **Share this book** with your family and friends to help spread the word about what's happening.

- **Leave a review** for this book online. It helps get the book promoted more through online sites.

- Influence your local politicians to end complicity and stand against genocide

- Support local municipalities to boycott companies that support grave human-rights violations

- Get involved with your local BDS movement

- Attend rallies and events in solidarity with Palestine

- Join local WhatsApp groups organized around political practices (signing petitions, sending letters, etc.)

---

1. https://youtu.be/1dQlFgMhxcI?si=aIK4YpsY3b6ul6n8&t=1910

• Pray for the people of Gaza and Palestine

• Avoid buying at or working for companies on The Witness' Boycott List[2]

Afterword

For additional sources, including multimedia information (images and videos), take a look at the following websites. Be advised that these videos are often the raw situation on the ground, and accordingly, may be graphic in nature.

- Justice For All's report on "Palestine—Genocide, Apartheid, and Occupation[1]"

- October 7 Fact Check[2], a continuously updated and thorough investigation of various statements related to the events and aftermath of October 7th.

- Stone Cold Justice: Israel's torture of Palestinian children - ABC Australia[3] (YouTube documentary)

- Reddit's /r/IsraelCrimes: https://www.reddit.com/r/IsraelCrimes/

- The Accountability Archive, on Twitter: https://twitter.com/archivegenocide

- Mohammed El Kurd, a writer from Jerusalem, on Instagram: https://www.instagram.com/mohammedelkurd/

- Plestia Alaqad, a journalist in Gaza, on Instagram: https://www.instagram.com/byplestia/

- The Witness, a UK-based newspaper, on Twitter: https://twitter.com/WitnessNewsUK

---

1. https://www.justiceforallcanada.org/pal-genocide.html

2. https://www.oct7factcheck.com/index

3. https://www.youtube.com/watch?v=cvOSv2fGJ5w&t=1820s

[1] "History of Palestine" by Wikipedia. Published December 25, 2008. Updated October 27, 2023. Accessed October 28, 2023. https://en.wikipedia.org/wiki/History_of_Palestine

[2] ibid

[3] ibid

[4] ibid

[5] ibid

[6] "Nakba" by Wikipedia. Published April 2, 2021. Updated October 28, 2023. Accessed October 28, 2023. https://en.wikipedia.org/wiki/Nakba

[7] ibid

[8] "The Nakba: 75 years after losing their home, the Palestinians are still experiencing the 'catastrophe'" by The Conversation. Published May 12, 2023. Accessed October 28, 2023. https://theconversation.com/the-nakba-75-years-after-losing-their-home-the-palestinians-are-still-experiencing-the-catastrophe-205413

[9] "Israel-Gaza war in maps and charts: Live tracker" by Al-Jazeera. Updated March 14, 2024. Published October 9, 2023. https://www.aljazeera.com/news/longform/2023/10/9/israel-hamas-war-in-maps-and-charts-live-tracker

[10] "Beheaded Babies" by October 7 Fact Check. Updated February 4, 2024. Accessed March 24, 2024. https://www.oct7factcheck.com/beheaded-babies

[11] "Baby found in Oven" by October 7 Fact Check. Updated January 16, 2024. Accessed March 24, 2024. https://www.oct7factcheck.com/baby-found-in-oven

[12] "Friendly fire - Israelis killed by IDF" by October 7 Fact Check. Updated February 21, 2024. Accessed March 24, 2024. https://www.oct7factcheck.com/oct7factcheck/Friendly-fire-Israelis-killed-by-IDF-a0b3530b556e423bb8b40f3b2a5e39bc

[13] "Child hostages kept in cages" by October 7 Fact Check. Updated February 18, 2024. Accessed March 24, 2024. https://www.oct7factcheck.com/child-hostages-kept-in-cages

[14] "800 scholars warn of potential genocide in Gaza" by Middle East Monitor. Published November 1, 2023. Accessed March 24, 2024. https://www.middleeastmonitor.com/20231101-800-scholars-warn-of-potential-genocide-in-gaza/

[15] "A top U.N. court says Gaza genocide is 'plausible' but does not order cease-fire" by NPR. Updated January 26, 2024. Accessed March 24, 2024. https://www.npr.org/2024/01/26/1227078791/icj-israel-genocide-gaza-palestinians-south-africa

[16] "Palestine—Genocide, Apartheid, and Occupation" by Justice for All. Published March 15, 2024. Retrieved March 24, 2024. https://www.justiceforallcanada.org/pal-genocide.html

[17] "Is What's Happening in Gaza a Genocide? Experts Weigh In" by TIME. Updated November 14, 2023. Retrieved March 24, 2024. https://time.com/6334409/is-whats-happening-gaza-genocide-experts/

[18] "Why Israel has been accused of committing genocide in Palestine" by Vox. Published November 13, 2023. Accessed March 24, 2024. https://www.vox.com/world-politics/2023/11/13/23954731/genocide-israel-gaza-palestine

[19] "Genocide case against Israel: Where does the rest of the world stand on the momentous allegations?" by AP News. Updated January 14, 2024. Retrieved March 24, 2024. https://apnews.com/article/genocide-israel-palestinians-gaza-court-fbd7fe4af10b542a1a4e2c7563029bfb

[20] "Experts, advocates deeply divided on question of 'genocide' in Gaza" by CBC News. Updated December 2, 2023. Retrieved March 24, 2024. https://www.cbc.ca/news/world/genocide-gaza-debate-1.7042809

[21] "Israel's 'war against Gaza's children' explained" by Al Jazeera. Published October 19, 2023. Accessed October 26, 2023. https://www.aljazeera.com/news/2023/10/19/israels-war-against-gazas-children-explained

[22] "First Intifada" by Wikipedia. Published August 14, 2002. Updated October 25, 2023. Accessed October 27, 2023. https://en.wikipedia.org/wiki/First_Intifada

[23] "Database on Fatalities and House Demolitions" by B'Tselem. Updated October 5, 2023. Accessed October 26, 2023. https://statistics.btselem.org/en/all-fatalities/by-date-of-incident?section=overall&tab=overview&ageSensor=%220%2C18%22

[24] "Israel-Gaza war in maps and charts: Live tracker" by Al-Jazeera. Updated 15 March, 2024. Published 0 October, 2023. https://www.aljazeera.com/news/longform/2023/10/9/israel-hamas-war-in-maps-and-charts-live-tracker

[25] "Palestine Genocide Apartheid & Occupation" by Justice for All, page 26. Published March 14, 2024. Accessed March 14, 2024. https://www.justiceforallcanada.org/pal-genocide.html

[26] "GAZA: More than 10 children a day lose a limb in three months of brutal conflict" by Save the Children. Published January 7, 2024. Accessed March 17, 2024. https://www.savethechildren.net/news/gaza-more-10-children-day-lose-limb-three-months-brutal-conflict

[27] "Stripped, beaten and blindfolded: new research reveals ongoing violence and abuse of Palestinian children detained by Israeli military" by Save the Children. Published July 10, 2023. Accessed March 23, 2024. https://www.savethechildren.net/news/stripped-beaten-and-blindfolded-new-research-reveals-ongoing-violence-and-abuse-palestinian[4]

[28] ibid

---

4. https://www.savethechildren.net/news/stripped-beaten-and-blindfolded new research-reveals-ongoing-violence-and-abuse-palestinian#

[29] "Stone Cold Justice: Israel's torture of Palestinian children - ABC Australia" on YouTube. Published February 10, 2021. Retrieved March 23, 2024. https://www.youtube.com/watch?v=cvOSv2fGJ5w&t=1820s

[30] "The Israelis threw a Palestinian boy in the oven, during the ethnic cleansing of Palestinians in 1948" by Syrian Girl on Twitter. Posted October 29, 2023. Retrieved March 23, 2023. https://twitter.com/Partisangirl/status/1718816122126966796

[31] "Deir Yassin makes a mockery of Israel's "never again" pledge" by The Electronic Intifada. Published April 8, 2022. Retrieved March 23, 2024. https://electronicintifada.net/content/deir-yassin-makes-mockery-israels-never-again-pledge/35176

[32] "Myth: The war of 1948 was inevitable self-defense for Israel" by Decolonize Palestine. Updated May 5, 2023. Retrieved March 23, 2024. https://decolonizepalestine.com/myth/the-war-of-1948-was-inevitable-self-defense-for-israel/

[33] "White flag executions by Israel" by October 7 Fact Check. Updated March 11, 2024. Retrieved March 24, 2024. https://www.oct7factcheck.com/oct7factcheck/White-flag-executions-by-Israel-5313b9bf8e82432e92abd6e61cef6963

[34] "Gaza: UN experts decry bombing of hospitals and schools as crimes against humanity, call for prevention of genocide" by the UN Human Rights Office. Published October 19, 2023. Accessed on October 20, 2023. https://www.ohchr.org/en/press-releases/2023/10/gaza-un-experts-decry-bombing-hospitals-and-schools-crimes-against-humanity

[35] "'Massacre': Dozens killed by Israeli fire in Gaza while collecting food aid" by Al Jazeera. Updated March 1, 2024. Accessed March 17, 2024. https://www.aljazeera.com/news/2024/2/29/dozens-killed-injured-by-israeli-fire-in-gaza-while-collecting-food-aid

[36] "Gaza: UN experts decry bombing of hospitals and schools as crimes against humanity, call for prevention of genocide" by the UN Human Rights Office. Published October 19, 2023. Accessed on October 20, 2023. https://www.ohchr.org/en/press-releases/2023/10/gaza-un-experts-decry-bombing-hospitals-and-schools-crimes-against-humanity

[37] "Israel-Palestine war: The Gaza civilian buildings bombed by Israeli army" by Middle East Eye. Published October 10, 2023. Accessed October 21, 2023. https://www.middleeasteye.net/news/israel-palestine-war-gaza-civilian-buildings-bombed

[38] ibid

[39] ibid

[40] ibid

[41] ibid

[42] ibid

[43] "Israel's destruction of multistorey buildings: extensive, wanton and unjustified" by Amnesty International. Published December 9, 2014. Accessed November 3, 2023. https://www.amnesty.org/en/latest/news/2014/12/israels-destruction-multistorey-buildings-extensive-wanton-and-unjustified/

[44] ibid

[45] ibid

[46]

[47] "Gaza humanitarian crisis (2023-present)" by Wikipedia. Updated March 19, 2024. Accessed March 23, 2024. https://en.wikipedia.org/wiki/Gaza_humanitarian_crisis_(2023%E2%80%93present)#Attacks_and_destruction

[48] "Israeli forces storm Gaza's al-Shifa Hospital" by Al Jazeera. Published March 18, 2024. Accessed March 23, 2024. https://www.aljazeera.com/news/2024/3/18/israeli-army-opens-fire-inside-gazas-al-shifa-hospital-officials-say

[49] ibid

[50] "Israel's war on Gaza live: Hundreds killed in al-Shifa Hospital siege" by Al Jazeera. Published March 31, 2024. Accessed March 31, 2024. https://www.aljazeera.com/news/liveblog/2024/3/31/israels-war-on-gaza-live-hundreds-killed-in-al-shifa-hospital-siege

[51] "Gaza humanitarian crisis (2023-present)" by Wikipedia. Updated March 19, 2024. Accessed March 23, 2024. https://en.wikipedia.org/wiki/Gaza_humanitarian_crisis_(2023%E2%80%93present)#Attacks_and_destruction

[52] "Israel-Palestine war: The Gaza civilian buildings bombed by Israeli army" by Middle East Eye. Published October 10, 2023. Accessed October 21, 2023. https://www.middleeasteye.net/news/israel-palestine-war-gaza-civilian-buildings-bombe[5]d[6]

[53] ibid

[54] ibid

[55] ibid

[56] "Gaza: UN experts decry bombing of hospitals and schools as crimes against humanity, call for prevention of genocide" by the UN Human Rights Office. Published October 19, 2023. Accessed on October 20, 2023. https://www.ohchr.org/en/press-releases/2023/10/gaza-un-experts-decry-bombing-hospitals-and-schools-crimes-against-humanity

[57] ibid

[58] ibid

[59] "Palestine Genocide Apartheid & Occupation" by Justice for All, page 26. Published March 14, 2024. Accessed March 14, 2024. https://www.justiceforallcanada.org/pal-genocide.html

---

5. https://www.middleeasteye.net/news/israel-palestine-war-gaza-civilian-buildings-bombed

6. https://www.middleeasteye.net/news/israel-palestine-war-gaza-civilian-buildings-bombed

[60] ibid

[61] "Warplanes Strike Gaza Refugee Camp as Israel Rejects U.S. Push for Pause in Fighting" by Time. Published November 5, 2023. Accessed November 5, 2023. https://time.com/6331653/gaza-refugee-camp-israel-hamas-war/

[62] "Israel accused of using controversial white phosphorus shells in Gaza amid war with Hamas" by CBS News. Published October 14, 2023. Accessed on October 20, 2023. https://www.cbsnews.com/news/israel-hamas-war-white-phosphorous-gaza-palestinians-amnesty-hrw-reports/

[63] "What is the white phosphorus that Israel is accused of using in Gaza?" by Al Jazeera. Published October 13, 2023. Accessed on October 20, 2023. https://www.aljazeera.com/news/2023/10/13/what-is-the-white-phosphorus-that-israel-is-accused-of-using-on-gaza

[64] ibid

[65] ibid

[66] "Israel: White Phosphorus Used in Gaza, Lebanon" by Human Rights Watch. Published October 12, 2023. Accessed on October 20, 2023. https://www.hrw.org/news/2023/10/12/israel-white-phosphorus-used-gaza-lebanon

[67] "What is the white phosphorus that Israel is accused of using in Gaza?" by Al Jazeera. Published October 13, 2023. Accessed on October 20, 2023. https://www.aljazeera.com/news/2023/10/13/what-is-the-white-phosphorus-that-israel-is-accused-of-using-on-gaza

[68] "Israel: White Phosphorus Used in Gaza, Lebanon" by Human Rights Watch. Published October 12, 2023. Accessed on October 20, 2023. https://www.hrw.org/news/2023/10/12/israel-white-phosphorus-used-gaza-lebanon

[69] " Rain of Fire: Israel's Unlawful Use of White Phosphorus in Gaza" by Human Rights Watch. Published March 25, 2009. Accessed March 23, 2024. https://www.hrw.org/report/2009/03/25/rain-fire/israels-unlawful-use-white-phosphorus-gaza

[70] "'We were baptised here and we will die here': Gaza's oldest church bombed" by Al Jazeera. Published October 20, 2023. Accessed October 30, 2023. https://www.aljazeera.com/features/2023/10/20/we-were-baptised-here-and-we-will-die-here-gazas-oldest-church-bombed

[71] ibid

[72] "UNRWA Says Five Killed, 22 Wounded in Israeli Strike on Gaza Food Distribution Center" by Tasnin News Agency. Published March 14, 2024. Accessed March 31, 2024. https://www.tasnimnews.com/en/news/2024/03/14/3054974/unrwa-says-five-killed-22-wounded-in-israeli-strike-on-gaza-food-distribution-center

[73] ibid

[74] "Israeli forces strike UN food center in Gaza, killing at least 5 people" by The Hill. Published March 13, 2024. Accessed March 31, 2024. https://thehill.com/homenews/ap/ap-top-headlines/ap-the-latest-palestinian-stabs-2-at-a-checkpoint-near-jerusalem-israeli-police-say/

[75] "Israeli torture in the occupied territories" by Wikipedia. Published February 9, 2019. Updated August 17, 2023. Accessed October 26, 2023. https://en.wikipedia.org/wiki/Israeli_torture_in_the_occupied_territories

[76] ibid

[77] "War Crimes in the Interrogation Chamber: The Israeli Systematic Policy of Torture, Inhuman and Degrading Treatment, Unlawful Deportation, and Denial of Fair Trial of Palestinian Detainees" by the Public Committee Against Torture in Israel. Published June, 2022. Accessed October 28, 2023. https://www.fidh.org/IMG/pdf/fidh-pcati_art__15_communication_palestine_crimes_isa.pdf

[78] ibid

[79]"Israeli torture in the occupied territories" by Wikipedia. Published February 9, 2019. Updated August 17, 2023. Accessed October 26, 2023. https://en.wikipedia.org/wiki/Israeli_torture_in_the_occupied_territories

[80] "At least 16 cemeteries in Gaza have been desecrated by Israeli forces, satellite imagery and videos reveal" by the Canadian National News. Published January 20, 2024. Accessed March 17, 2024. https://www.cnn.com/2024/01/20/middleeast/israel-gaza-cemeteries-desecrated-investigation-intl-cmd/index.html

[81] "Stop evictions in East Jerusalem neighbourhood immediately, UN rights office urges Israel" by UN News. Published May 7, 2021. Accessed on October 20, 2023. https://news.un.org/en/story/2021/05/1091492

[82] ibid

[83] ibid

[84] "UN independent experts spotlight 'prima facie war crime' in East Jerusalem" by UN News. Published April 13, 2021. Accessed on October 20, 2023. https://news.un.org/en/story/2023/04/1135602

[85] "Chemical attacks by Israel threaten Gaza's agriculture, farm workers' health" by Yeni Safak. Published March 21, 2024. Accessed March 23, 2024. https://www.yenisafak.com/en/news/chemical-attacks-by-israel-threaten-gazas-agriculture-farm-workers-health-3679786

[86] "Israel poisoning soil by using banned munitions in Gaza: Palestinian official" by Yeni Safak. Published March 21, 2024. Accessed March 23, 2024. https://www.yenisafak.com/en/news/israel-poisoning-soil-by-using-banned-munitions-in-gaza-palestinian-official-3679816

[87] "Adalah, Gisha, and Al Mezan seek redress for Gaza farmers' losses due to Israeli military spraying of their land" by Al Mezan Center for Human Rights. Published August 1st, 2016. Accessed via the Internet Archive on October 21, 2023. http://web.archive.org/web/20220528192823/http://mezan.org/en/post/21468

[88] "Israel's herbicide spraying: Palestinian farmers' means of subsistence jeopardised" by Euromed Rights. Published April 22, 2020. Accessed October 21, 2023. https://euromedrights.org/publication/israels-herbicide-spraying-palestinian-farmers-means-of-subsistence-jeopardised[7]

[89] "Adalah, Gisha, and Al Mezan seek redress for Gaza farmers' losses due to Israeli military spraying of their land" by Al Mezan Center for Human Rights. Published August 1st, 2016. Accessed via the Internet Archive on October 21, 2023. http://web.archive.org/web/20220528192823/http://mezan.org/en/post/21468

[90] "Israel's herbicide spraying: Palestinian farmers' means of subsistence jeopardised" by Euromed Rights. Published April 22, 2020. Accessed October 21, 2023. https://euromedrights.org/publication/israels-herbicide-spraying-palestinian-farmers-means-of-subsistence-jeopardised[8]

[91] ibid

[92] "Israeli spraying of herbicide near Gaza harming Palestinian crops" by The Guardian. Published September 6, 2019. Accessed October 21, 2023. https://www.theguardian.com/world/2019/jul/19/israeli-spraying-of-herbicide-near-gaza-harming-palestinian-crops

[93] "War crime? Israel destroys Gaza crops with aerial herbicide spraying" by the Ecologist. Published February 18, 2016. Accessed November 5, 2023. https://theecologist.org/2016/feb/18/war-crime-israel-destroys-gaza-crops-aerial-herbicide-spraying

[94] ibid

[95] "Adalah, Gisha, and Al Mezan seek redress for Gaza farmers' losses due to Israeli military spraying of their land" by Al Mezan Center for Human Rights. Published August 1st, 2016. Accessed via the Internet Archive on October 21, 2023. http://web.archive.org/web/20220528192823/http://mezan.org/en/post/21468

---

7. https://euromedrights.org/publication/israels-herbicide-spraying-palestinian-farmers-means-of-subsistence-jeopardised/

8. https://euromedrights.org/publication/israels-herbicide-spraying-palestinian-farmers-means-of-subsistence-jeopardised/

[96] "Israel's herbicide spraying: Palestinian farmers' means of subsistence jeopardised" by Euromed Rights. Published April 22, 2020. Accessed October 21, 2023. https://euromedrights.org/publication/israels-herbicide-spraying-palestinian-farmers-means-of-subsistence-jeopardised[9]

[97] "Video Shows Israelis Filling Palestinians' Water Source With Concrete?" by Snopes. Published March 22, 2024. Retrieved March 23, 2024. https://www.snopes.com/fact-check/israelis-filling-water-with-concrete/

[98] ibid

[99] "Gaza electricity crisis" by Wikipedia. Published June 4, 2017. Updated October 26, 2023. Accessed October 27, 2023. https://en.wikipedia.org/wiki/Gaza_electricity_crisis

[100] "Energy in the State of Palestine" by Wikipedia. Published June 13, 2015. Updated June 26, 2023. Accessed October 26, 2023. https://en.wikipedia.org/wiki/Energy_in_the_State_of_Palestine

[101] ibid

[102] "Israel: Immediately Restore Electricity, Water, Aid to Gaza" by Human Rights Watch. Published October 21, 2023. Accessed October 27, 2023. https://www.hrw.org/news/2023/10/21/israel-immediately-restore-electricity-water-aid-gaza

[103] "Gaza electricity crisis" by Wikipedia. Published June 4, 2017. Updated October 26, 2023. Accessed October 27, 2023. https://en.wikipedia.org/wiki/Gaza_electricity_crisis

[104] ibid

[105] "World Report 2022: Israel and Palestine" by Human Rights Watch. Updated April 11, 2022. Accessed October 27, 2023. https://www.hrw.org/world-report/2022/country-chapters/israel-and-palestine

---

9. https://euromedrights.org/publication/israels-herbicide-spraying-palestinian-farmers-means-of-subsistence-jeopardised/

[106] "Why is Gaza out of fuel — and what now?" by Al Jazeera, Published October 11, 2023. Accessed October 27, 2023. https://www.aljazeera.com/news/2023/10/11/why-is-gaza-out-of-fuel-and-what

[107] "October 27, 2023 Israel-Hamas war news" by CNN. Updated October 28, 2023. Accessed October 28, 2203. https://edition.cnn.com/middleeast/live-news/israel-hamas-war-gaza-news-10-27-23/h_8b3a7203e2fd228167f5dcbd3c44764b

[108] "Palestinians Report Total Communication Blackout as Israel Expands Ground Operation" by Time Magazine. Published October 27, 2023. Accessed October 28, 2023. https://time.com/6329388/israel-palestine-gaza-strip-communication-blackout/

[109] ibid

[110] ibid

[111] "Israel defends Gaza internet blackout" by The Telegraph. Published October 28, 2023. Retrieved October 28, 2023. https://www.telegraph.co.uk/world-news/2023/10/28/israel-gaza-latest-news-updates-hamas-palestine-day-22-live/

[112] "Gaza: Un experts condemn killing and silencing of journalists" by the UN Human Rights Office of the High Commissioner. Published February 1, 2024. https://www.ohchr.org/en/press-releases/2024/02/ga-za-un-experts-condemn-killing-and-silencing-journalists

[113] "Palestine Genocide Apartheid & Occupation" by Justice for All, page 26. Published March 14, 2024. Accessed March 14, 2024. https://www.justiceforallcanada.org/pal-genocide.html

[114] "Journalist casualties in the Israel-Gaza conflict" by Committee to Protect Journalists. Updated March 17, 2024. Accessed March 17, 2024. https://cpj.org/2023/10/journalist-casualties-in-the-israel-gaza-conflict/

[115] ibid

[116] "At least 24 journalists have been killed in the war between Israel and Hamas in Gaza" by NPR. Updated October 26, 2023. Accessed October 27, 2023. https://www.npr.org/2023/10/25/1208019720/journalist-deaths-gaza-israel-hamas

[117] ibid

[118] "Death of José Andrés' World Central Kitchen crew marks a new low in Gaza war, aid workers say" by USA Today. Updated April 4, 2024. Accessed April 6, 2024. https://www.usatoday.com/story/news/world/2024/04/03/jose-andres-world-central-kitchen-workers-killed-gaza/73185006007/

[119] "Fact Sheet: The Killing of Rachel Corrie" by the Institute for Middle-East Understanding. Published March 15, 2023. Retrieved March 21, 2024. https://imeu.org/article/fact-sheet-the-killing-of-rachel-corrie-ten-years-later

[120] ibid

[121] "'Women in Gaza are being raped and this is not being investigated or reported'" by Middle East Monitor. Published March 24, 2024. Retrieved April 6, 2024. https://www.middleeastmonitor.com/20240324-women-in-gaza-are-being-raped-and-this-is-not-being-investigated-or-reported/

[122] "Israeli torture in the occupied territories" by Wikipedia. Published February 9, 2019. Updated August 17, 2023. Accessed October 26, 2023. https://en.wikipedia.org/wiki/Israeli_torture_in_the_occupied_territories

[123] ibid

[124] "Attacks, arrests, threats, censorship: The high risks of reporting the Israel-Hamas war" by the Committee to Protect Journalists. Published October 27, 2023. Accessed October 27, 2023. https://cpj.org/2023/10/attacks-arrests-threats-censorship-the-high-risks-of-reporting-the-israel-hamas-war/

[125] ibid

[126] "CPJ calls on Israeli authorities to protect press freedom, journalist safety amid Israeli-Palestinian conflict" by the Committee to Protect Journalists. Published May 14, 2021. Accessed October 26, 2023. https://cpj.org/2021/05/cpj-calls-on-israeli-authorities-to-protect-press-freedom-journalist-safety-amid-israeli-palestinian-conflict/

[127] ibid

[128] "CPJ calls on Israeli authorities to protect press freedom, journalist safety amid Israeli-Palestinian conflict" by the Committee to Protect Journalists. Published May 14, 2021. Accessed October 26, 2023. https://cpj.org/2021/05/cpj-calls-on-israeli-authorities-to-protect-press-freedom-journalist-safety-amid-israeli-palestinian-conflict/

[129] "Attacks, arrests, threats, censorship: The high risks of reporting the Israel-Hamas war" by the Committee to Protect Journalists. Published October 27, 2023. Accessed October 27, 2023. https://cpj.org/2023/10/attacks-arrests-threats-censorship-the-high-risks-of-reporting-the-israel-hamas-war/

[130] ibid

[131] "Israel/OPT: Appalling Gaza 'evacuation order' must be rescinded by Israel immediately" by Amnesty International. Published October 13, 2023. Accessed on October 20, 2023. https://www.amnesty.org/en/latest/news/2023/10/israel-opt-appalling-gaza-evacuation-order-must-be-rescinded-by-israel-immediately/

[132] "Israel seizes 800 hectares of Palestinian land in occupied West Bank" by Al Jazeera. Published March 22, 2024. Retrieved March 23, 2024. https://www.aljazeera.com/news/2024/3/22/israel-seizes-800-hectares-of-palestinian-land-in-occupied-west-bank

[133] "Land expropriation in the West Bank" by Wikipedia. Updated March 16, 2024. Retrieved March 23, 2024. https://en.wikipedia.org/wiki/Land_expropriation_in_the_West_Bank

[134] "By Hook and by Crook: Israeli Settlement Policy in the West Bank" by B'Tselem. Published July 2010. Retrieved March 23, 2024. https://www.btselem.org/publications/summaries/201007_by_hook_and_by_crook

[135] "Israel's Occupation: 50 Years of Dispossession" by Amnesty International. Published June 7, 2017. Retrieved March 23, 2024. https://www.amnesty.org/en/latest/campaigns/2017/06/israel-occupation-50-years-of-dispossession/

[136] "International law and Israeli settlements" by Wikipedia. Updated August 30, 2023. Accessed October 25, 2023. https://en.wikipedia.org/wiki/International_law_and_Israeli_settlements

[137] "Doing Business in the Illegal Israeli Settlements? Think Twice" by Amnesty International. Published July 9, 2019. Accessed on October 20, 2023. https://amnesty.ca/corporate-accountability/doing-business-in-the-illegal-israeli-settlements-think-twice/

[138] "UN General Assembly ADOPTS resolution on "protection of civilians and upholding legal and humanitarian obligations" on the ongoing Gaza crisis" by UN News. Published October 27, 2023. Accessed October 30, 2023. https://twitter.com/UN_News_Centre/status/1717992371906839005

[139] "Israeli forces move further into Gaza as Netanyahu declares 'time for war'" by Al Jazeera. Published October 30, 2023. Accessed October 30, 2023. https://www.aljazeera.com/news/2023/10/30/israeli-forces-move-further-into-gaza-as-netanyahu-declares-time-for-war

[140] ibid

[141] "Warplanes Strike Gaza Refugee Camp as Israel Rejects U.S. Push for Pause in Fighting" by Time. Published November 5, 2023. Accessed November 5, 2023. https://time.com/6331653/gaza-refugee-camp-israel-hamas-war/

[142] "Destruction of Palestinian olive trees is a monstrous crime" by the Ecologist. Published November 7, 2015. Accessed November 1, 2023. https://theecologist.org/2015/nov/07/destruction-palestinian-olive-trees-monstrous-crime

[143] "Bitter harvest in West Bank's olive groves" by The Guardian. Published November 14, 2003. Accessed November 1, 2023. https://www.theguardian.com/world/2003/nov/14/israel

[144] "Destruction of Palestinian olive trees is a monstrous crime" by the Ecologist. Published November 7, 2015. Accessed November 1, 2023. https://theecologist.org/2015/nov/07/destruction-palestinian-olive-trees-monstrous-crime

[145] ibid

[146] "9,300 olive trees destroyed by Israel in the West Bank in one year, says ICRC" by Middle East Monitor. Published October 13, 2021. Accessed November 1, 2023. https://www.middleeastmonitor.com/20211013-9300-olive-trees-destroyed-by-israel-in-the-west-bank-in-one-year-says-icrc/

[147] Ibid

[148] ibid

[149] "Real Video of Israeli Protesters Dancing to Rave Music While Blocking Aid to Gaza?" by Snopes. Published February 14, 2024. Retrieved March 23, 2024. https://www.snopes.com/fact-check/israeli-protesters-aid-gaza/?cb_rec=djRfMl8xXzRfMTgwXzBfMF8wXw

[150] "Gaza: Israel's 'Open-Air Prison' at 15" by Human Rights Watch. Published June 14, 2022. Accessed October 25, 2023. https://www.hrw.org/news/2022/06/14/gaza-israels-open-air-prison-15

[151] ibid

[152] "How Gaza became an open air prison" by Slate. Published October 16, 2023. Accessed October 21, 2023. https://slate.com/news-and-politics/2023/10/how-gaza-became-an-open-air-prison.html

[153] ibid

[154] "Palestinians Can't Just Leave Gaza During Israel-Hamas Conflict" by Bloomberg News. Published October 12, 2023. Accessed October 21, 2023. https://www.bloomberg.com/opinion/articles/2023-10-12/palestinians-can-t-just-leave-gaza-during-israel-hamas-conflict#xj4y7vzkg

[155] ibid

[156] ibid

[157] ibid

[158] ibid

[159] ibid

[160] ibid

[161] ibid

[162] "Israel's apartheid against Palestinians: a cruel system of domination and a crime against humanity" by Amnesty International. Published February 1, 2022. Accessed October 28, 2023. https://www.amnesty.org/en/latest/news/2022/02/israels-apartheid-against-palestinians-a-cruel-system-of-domination-and-a-crime-against-humanity/

[163] "Israel's Apartheid against Palestinians" by Amnesty International. Accessed October 27, 2023. https://www.amnesty.org/en/latest/campaigns/2022/02/israels-system-of-apartheid/

[164] ibid

[165] ibid

[166] "Israel's occupation of Palestinian Territory is 'apartheid': UN rights expert" by United Nations News. Published March 25, 2022. Accessed October 27, 2023. https://news.un.org/en/story/2022/03/1114702

[167] ibid

[168] ibid

[169] "Top UN official in New York steps down citing 'genocide' of Palestinian civilians" by The Guardian. Published October 31, 2023. Accessed November 3, 2023. https://www.theguardian.com/world/2023/oct/31/un-official-resigns-israel-hamas-war-palestine-new-york

[170] ibid

[171] ibid

[172] "Racism in Israel" by Wikipedia. Published June 18, 2022. Updated October 25, 2023. https://en.wikipedia.org/wiki/
Racism_in_Israel#Racism_against_Arab_citizens_by_Israeli_Jews

[173] "Anti-Arab Racism" by Wikipedia. Published July 29, 2002. Accessed October 30, 2023.. https://en.wikipedia.org/wiki/Anti-Arab_racism#Israel

[174] https://en.wikipedia.org/wiki/Anti-Arab_racism#Israel

[175] "Racism in Israel" by Wikipedia. Published June 18, 2022. Updated October 25, 2023. https://en.wikipedia.org/wiki/
Racism_in_Israel#Racism_against_Arab_citizens_by_Israeli_Jews

[176] ibid

[177] https://en.wikipedia.org/wiki/Anti-Arab_racism#Israel

[178] ibid

[179] ibid

[180] "Racism in Israel" by Wikipedia. Published June 18, 2022. Updated October 25, 2023. https://en.wikipedia.org/wiki/
Racism_in_Israel#Racism_against_Arab_citizens_by_Israeli_Jews

[181] "ibid

[182] ibid

[183] ibid

[184] ibid

[185] https://en.wikipedia.org/wiki/Anti-Arab_racism#Israel

[186] ibid

[187] "Overview of Anti-Democratic Legislation Advanced by the 20th Knesset" by The Association for Civil Rights in Israel. Published in 2018. Accessed October 30, 2023. https://law.acri.org.il/en/wp-content/uploads/2018/10/Overview-of-Anti-Democratic-Legislation-October-2018.pdf

[188] "Israel's Vaccine Discrimination against Palestinians Must End" by Physicians for Human Rights. Published March 15, 2021. Accessed November 6, 2023. https://phr.org/our-work/resources/israels-vaccine-discrimination-against-palestinians-must-end/

[189] ibid

[190] " UN experts call on Israel to ensure equal access to COVID-19 vaccines for Palestinians" by UN Office of Human Rights. Published January 14, 2021. Accessed November 6, 2023. https://www.ohchr.org/en/press-releases/2021/01/israelopt-un-experts-call-israel-ensure-equal-access-covid-19-vaccines?LangID=E&NewsID=26655

[191] "The Six Grave Violations" by the Office of the Special Representative of the Secretary-General for Children and Armed Conflict. Accessed November 3, 2023. https://childrenandarmedconflict.un.org/six-grave-violations/

[192] "Grave violations against Palestinian children: October 27" by Defense for Children Palestine. Published October 27, 2023. Accessed November 3, 2023. https://www.dci-palestine.org/ grave_violations_against_palestinian_children_in_gaza_october_27

[193] ibid

[194] Tweet by WikiLeaks on Twitter. Published October 30, 2023. Accessed November 3, 2023. https://twitter.com/wikileaks/status/ 1719000849299407012?s=48&t=zGUGyf3Km0nbROe9bwTdXA

[195] "e complete document of the Ministry of Intelligence: occupation of Gaza and total transfer to its residents" by Mekomit. Published October 28, 2023. Accessed November 3, 2023. Translated by Google Translate. https://www.mekomit.co.il/%D7%94%D7%9E%D7%A1%D7%9E%D7%9A-%D7%94%D7%9E

[196] ibid

[197] ibid

[198] ibid

[199] "World Report 2022: Israel and Palestine" by Human Rights Watch. Updated April 11, 2022. Accessed October 27, 2023. https://www.hrw.org/world-report/2022/ country-chapters/israel-and-palestine

[200] ibid

[201] "Statistics on Palestinians in Israeli custody" by B'Tselem. Updated September 7, 2023. Accessed October 26, 2023. https://www.btselem.org/statistics/detainees_and_prisoners

[202] "Statistics on Palestinian minors in Israeli custody" by B'Tselem. Updated September 7, 2023. Accessed October 26, 2023. https://www.btselem.org/statistics/minors_in_custody

[203] "Statistics on administrative detention in the Occupied Territories" by B'Tselem. Updated September 7, 2023. Accessed October 26, 2023. https://www.btselem.org/administrative_detention/statistics

[204] "Doing Business in the Illegal Israeli Settlements? Think Twice." by Amnesty International. Published July 9, 2019. Accessed November 6, 2023. https://amnesty.ca/corporate-accountability/doing-business-in-the-illegal-israeli-settlements-think-twice/

[205] "World Report 2022: Israel and Palestine" by Human Rights Watch. Updated April 11, 2022. Accessed October 27, 2023. https://www.hrw.org/world-report/2022/country-chapters/israel-and-palestine

[206] "Database of Palestine colonization quotes - PALCIT" by PALCIT. Accessed October 26, 2023. https://palcit.net/

[207] Ibid

[208] "The old will die and the young will forget" by David Ben Gurion. Published by Arab News. Published April 25, 2002. Accessed October 21, 2023. https://www.arabnews.com/node/220313

[209] Quotation from Eliezer Bauer, by PALCIT. Accessed October 26, 2023. https://palcit.net/article-1417-when-adult-males-were-discovered-hiding...-they-were-killed

[210] Bauer to Galili, Moshe Mann, Baruch Rabinov and Yaakov Riftin, Eliezer Bauer Papers. Cited by Benny Morris, The Birth of the Palestinian Problem Revisited, Cambridge Univ. Press, 2005, p. 242

[211] Quotation from David Ben Gurion, by PALCIT. Accessed October 26, 2023. https://palcit.net/article-905-as-april-began-our-war-of-independence-swung-decisively-from-defense-to-attack

[212] Ben Gurion, Rebirth and Destiny of Israel N.Y.: Philosophical Library, 1954, p. 106.

[213] Quotation from Quotation from Leo Heiman, by PALCIT. Accessed October 26, 2023. https://palcit.net/article-926-save-your-souls-all-ye-faithful-the-jews-are-using-poison-gas-and-atomic-weapons

[214] Quotation from Yigal Allon, by PALCIT. Accessed October 26, 2023. https://palcit.net/article-930-achieve-total-victory-the-territorial-fulfillment-of-the-land-of-israel

[215] Benny Morris, *Victimes. Histoire revisitée du conflit arabo-sioniste*, Complexe, 2003, p.351 ; Sylvain Cypel. *Les emmurés*, La Découverte, 2005, p. 200.

[216] Quotation from Moshe Dayan, by PALCIT. Accessed October 26, 2023. https://palcit.net/article-960-not-one-single-place-built-that-did-not-have-a-former-arab-population

[217] Speech at the Technion, Haifa, Haaretz, April 4 1969.

[218] Ibid DBG

[219] Quotation from Golda Meir, by PALCIT. Accessed October 26, 2023. https://palcit.net/article-955-for-me-the-supreme-morality-is-the-the-jewish-people-has-a-right-to-exist

[220] Benny Morris *Victimes, Histoire revisitée du conflir arabo-sioniste,* Complexes, 2003, p. 374.

[221] Ibid DBG

[222] "Israeli Prime Ministers who were Terrorists and War Criminals" by The Hypertexts. Accessed October 25, 2023. http://www.thehypertexts.com/Israeli%20Prime%20Ministers%20Terrorists%20Nakba.htm

[223] Ibid DBG

[224] Quotation from Yoram Ben Porath, by PALCIT. Accessed October 25, 2023. https://palcit.net/article-979-there-is-no-zionism-...without-the-eviction-of-the-arabs-and-the-expropriation-of-their-lands

[225] Yediot Aharonot, July 14, 1972.

[226] Ibid DBG

[227] Quotation from Yitzhak Rabin, by PALCIT. Accessed October 26, 2023. https://palcit.net/article-868-ben-gurion-waved-his-hand-in-a-gesture-which-said-drive-them-out

[228] Yitzhak Rabin, New York Times, October 23 1979.

[229] Quotation from Golda Meir, by PALCIT. Accessed October 26, 2023. https://palcit.net/article-1001-all-the-arabs-are-the-same.-they-should-all-be-finished-off

[230] Abba Eban, Morality and warfare, The Jerusalem Post, August 16, 1981, cited in Edward Herman, The Real Terror Network, (Montreal: Black Rose Books, 1982), p. 77.

[231] Quotation from Abba Eban, by PALCIT. Accessed October 26, 2023. https://palcit.net/article-1364-israel-wantonly-inflicting-every-possible-measure-of-death

[232] Abba Eban, Morality and warfare, The Jerusalem Post, August 16, 1981, cited in Edward Herman, The Real Terror Network, (Montreal: Black Rose Books, 1982), p. 77.

[233] Ibid DBG

[234] "On Palestine: Victor Davis Hanson, Jordan Peterson and Bobby Kennedy Jr. — Profiles in Cowardice" by Michael Hoffman. Published October 8, 2023. Accessed October 26, 2023. https://michaelhoffman.substack.com/p/on-palestine-victor-davis-hanson

[235] Quotation from UN / ONU, by PALCIT. Accessed October 26, 2023. https://palcit.net/article-1032-to-gain-control-of-the-area-allotted-to-the-jewish-state-and-blocs-outside-those-borders

[236] Nathaniel Lorch, *The Edge of the Sword: Israel's War of Independence* , 1947-1949 (New York, Putnam, 1961), p. 87.

[237] Quotation from Arieh Biro, by PALCIT. Accessed October 26, 2023. https://palcit.net/article-1045-there-was-no-choice-but-to-kill-them.-this-is-not-such-a-big-deal

[238] The New York Times, Aug. 21, 1995.

[239] Quotation from Edward Said, by PALCIT. Accessed October 26, 2023. https://palcit.net/article-1059-drop-by-drop-tactic-in-which-one-or-two-houses-are-demolished-daily

[240] Edward Said, After the final acre , Al-Ahram, n° 387, 23-25.7.1998

[241] Ibid DBG

[242] Quotation from Ariel Sharon, by PALCIT. Accessed October 26, 2023. https://palcit.net/article-1061-everything-that-s-grabbed-will-be-in-our-hands

[243] AFP, Nov. 15, 1998

[244] Quotation from Ariel Sharon, by PALCIT. Accessed October 26, 2023.https://palcit.net/article-1073-no-one-has-the-right-to-put-the-jewish-people-and-the-state-of-israel-on-trial

[245] "Clashes mar Mid-East inquiry," by BBC News. Published March 25, 2001. Accessed October 26, 2023. http://news.bbc.co.uk/2/hi/middle_east/1241371.stm

[246] Quotation from Yitzhak Frankenthal, by PALCIT. Accessed October 26, 2023. https://palcit.net/article-1087-they-have-been-ready-to-make-peace-with-us-it-is-we-who-are-unwilling

[247] "I would have done the same," by The Guardian. Published August 7, 2002. Accessed October 26, 2023. https://www.theguardian.com/world/2002/aug/07/comment

[248] Quotation from Yitzhak Pundak, by PALCIT. Accessed October 26, 2023. https://palcit.net/article-1110-we-had-to-destroy-them-otherwise-we-would-have-had-arabs-here

[249] Haaretz, Pundak, May 21 2004. As quoted by Ilan Pappe, *The Ethnic Cleansing of Palestine* , One World Publications, 2006, p.6.

[250] Quotation from Efraim Eitam, by PALCIT. Accessed October 26, 2023. https://palcit.net/article-1111-we-will-have-to-kill-them-all

[251] "Among the Settlers" by The New Yorker. Published May 24, 2004. Accessed October 26, 2023. https://www.newyorker.com/magazine/2004/05/31/among-the-settlers

[252] Quotation from Ehud Olmert, by PALCIT. Accessed October 26, 2023. https://palcit.net/article-1368-commanders-and-soldiers-are-safe-from-tribunals

[253] "Israel prepares legal defense of soldiers" by CNN. Published January 25, 2009. Accessed October 26, 2023. http://edition.cnn.com/2009/WORLD/meast/01/25/gaza.legal.defense/

[254] Quotation from Ariel Atias, by PALCIT. Accessed October 26, 2023. https://palcit.net/article-1139-a-national-duty-to-prevent-the-spread-of-a-population-that-does-not-love-israel

[255] Ben White, Palestinians in Israel, pp. 54-55. Etre palestinien en Israël , La Guillotine, 2015.

[256] Quotation from Yitzhak Shapira, by PALCIT. Accessed October 26, 2023.https://palcit.net/article-1251-there-is-a-reason-to-kill-babies

[257] Matthiew Wagner. Book advocating killing gentiles who endanger Jews is hard to come by Jerusalem Post, Nov. 11, 2009.

[258] Quotation from Eli Yishai, by PALCIT. Accessed October 26, 2023.https://palcit.net/article-1377-we-must-blow-gaza-back-to-the-middle-ages

[259] The Yeshiva World News, LIVE BLOG DAY 4: Operation Pillar of Defense, November 17, 2012

[260] Quotation from Moshe Feiglin, by PALCIT. Accessed October 26, 2023.https://palcit.net/article-1163-i-ve-killed-lots-of-arabs-in-my-life-and-there-s-no-problem-with-that

[261] "Bennett under fire for comments about killing Arabs" by The Jerusalem Post. Published July 30, 2013. Accessed October 26, 2023. https://www.jpost.com/diplomacy-and-politics/bennett-under-fire-for-comments-about-killing-arabs-321467

[262] Quotation from Uri Elitzur, by PALCIT. Accessed October 26, 2023. https://palcit.net/article-1178-what-s-so-horrifying-about-understanding-that-the-entire-palestinian-people-is-the-enemy

[263] Quotation from Ayelet Shaked, by PALCIT. Accessed October 26, 2023. https://palcit.net/article-1179-the-entire-palestinian-people-are-the-enemy-including-its-elderly-and-its-women

[264] "Israeli lawmaker's call for genocide of Palestinians gets thousands of Facebook likes" by The Electronic Intifada. Published July 7, 2014. Updated May 8, 2015. Accessed October 26, 2023. https://electronicintifada.net/blogs/ali-abunimah/israeli-lawmakers-call-genocide-palestinians-gets-thousands-facebook-likes

[265] Quotation from Moshe Feiglin, by PALCIT. Accessed October 26, 2023. https://palcit.net/article-1379-gaza-will-become-part-of-sovereign-israel

[266] "My Outline for a Solution in Gaza" by Israel National News. Published July 15, 2014. Accessed October 26, 2023. http://www.israelnationalnews.com/news/343914

[267] Quotation from Avigdor Lieberman, by PALCIT. Accessed October 26, 2023.https://palcit.net/article-1186-those-who-are-against-us-...we-need-to-pick-up-an-ax-and-cut-off-his-head

[268] "Lieberman: Disloyal Israeli Arabs Should Be Beheaded" by Haaretz. Published March 9, 2015. Accessed October 26, 2023. https://www.haaretz.com/2015-03-09/ty-article/lieberman-disloyal-israeli-arabs-should-be-beheaded/0000017f-ee63-d4cd-af7f-ef7bba370000

[269] Quotation from Ayelet Shaked, by PALCIT. Accessed October 26, 2023. https://palcit.net/article-1331-maintain-a-jewish-majority-even-at-the-price-of-violation-of-rights

[270] "Justice Minister: Israel Must Keep Jewish Majority Even at the Expense of Human Rights" by Haaretz. Published February 13, 2018. Accessed October 26, 2023. https://www.haaretz.com/israel-news/2018-02-13/ty-article/justice-minister-israels-jewish-majority-trumps-than-human-rights/0000017f-e76d-d97e-a37f-f76d21180000

[271] "Top Israeli minister: 'No such thing' as Palestinian people," by Los Angeles Times. Published March 20, 2023. Accessed October 26, 2023. https://www.latimes.com/world-nation/story/2023-03-20/top-israeli-minister-no-such-thing-as-palestinian-people

[272] "The language being used to describe Palestinians is genocidal," by The Guardian. Published October 16, 2023. Retrieved October 28, 2023. https://www.theguardian.com/commentisfree/2023/oct/16/the-language-being-used-to-describe-palestinians-is-genocidal

[273] "Defense minister announces 'complete siege' of Gaza: No power, food or fuel" by the Times of Israel. Published October 9, 2023. Accessed October 23, 2023. https://www.timesofisrael.com/liveblog_entry/defense-minister-announces-complete-siege-of-gaza-no-power-food-or-fuel/

[274] Israeli Lawmaker Calls for "Doomsday Weapon" to "Level Gaza Without Mercy", by the New American. Published October 13, 2023. Accessed October 28, 2023. https://thenewamerican.com/world-news/middle-east/israeli-lawmaker-calls-for-doomsday-weapon-to-level-gaza-without-mercy/

[275] Twitter post by author. Published October 10, 2023. Accessed October 28, 2023. Translated by Google Translate. https://twitter.com/TallyGotliv/status/1711678420235534705

[276] "COGAT chief addresses Gazans: 'You wanted hell, you will get hell'" by the Times of Israel. Published October 10, 2023. Accessed October 28, 2023. https://www.timesofisrael.com/liveblog_entry/cogat-chief-addresses-gazans-you-wanted-hell-you-will-get-hell/

[277] "'A Massive War Crime': Israel Announces Total Blockade of Gaza Strip" by Common Dreams. Published October 9, 2023. Accessed October 23, 2023. https://www.commondreams.org/news/israel-blockade-gaza

[278] "As the World Watches the Growing Death Toll in Gaza and Israel" by Havana Times. Published October 9, 2023. Accessed October 28, 2023. https://havanatimes.org/news/as-the-world-watches-the-growing-death-toll-in-gaza-and-israel/

[279] ibid

[280] "Israel-Palestine war: Israeli veteran, 95, rallies troops to 'erase' Palestinian children" by the Middle East Eye. Published October 14, 2023. Accessed October 28, 2023. https://www.middleeasteye.net/news/israel-palestine-war-veteran-ezra-yachin-soldiers-erase-children

[281] "Moshe Feiglin: The only solution is the "complete destruction of Gaza" by Middle East Eye. Published October 26, 2023. Accessed March 17, 2024. https://www.youtube.com/watch?v=rjLW847tvig

[282] "Former Israeli ambassador to UN calls Palestinians 'horrible, inhuman animals'" by Al Arabiya News. Published October 26, 2023. Retrieved March 17, 2024. https://english.alarabiya.net/News/middle-east/2023/10/26/Former-Israeli-ambassador-to-UN-calls-Palestinians-horrible-inhuman-animals-

[283] "Israeli politician: 'The children of Gaza have brought this upon themselves'" by Mondoweiss. Published October 18, 2023. Retrieved March 24, 2024. https://mondoweiss.net/2023/10/israeli-politician-the-children-of-gaza-have-brought-this-upon-themselves/